THE PAIN
AND
THE GLORY

THE PAIN
AND
THE GLORY

Photographs by
Scott Mitchell
Words by
Sarah Edworthy
Introduction by
Dave Brailsford

Harper
Sport

INTRODUCTION 006
THE STORY OF THE GIRO 008
THE GIRO IN DETAIL 092
THE STORY OF THE TOUR 116
THE TOUR IN DETAIL 200

CONTENTS

Coming into Paris in the dark to seal our second successive Tour de France victory was different, that's for sure – a special moment to savour. It was a brilliant story last year when Bradley Wiggins became the first Briton to win the greatest prize in cycling, but to return with a different leader and win in consecutive years, in the historic 100th edition of the race, created a deep sense of achievement for everyone at Team Sky.

From the outside, those three weeks that Chris Froome ultimately dominated might have looked controlled, but from the inside they felt pretty epic. After the first Pyrenean stage, during which strong teamwork enabled Chris to show his superiority, something dramatic happened every single day. There was a tremendous sense of pride for the behind-the-scenes staff in witnessing the spectacle when the riders crossed the line with linked arms on the Champs-Élysées. Going on a Grand Tour means living together 24/7 for almost four weeks. It's like a soap opera, with a real sense of shared endeavour and camaraderie. After being in that kind of rhythm, it was wonderful to celebrate the magnitude of the occasion as a team.

In 2010 we launched Team Sky as a professional road-racing outfit with the aim of a clean British rider winning the Tour de France within five years. I said last year that you couldn't script a more perfect way of realising this ambition than that moment on Sunday 22 July 2012, when Mark Cavendish won on the Champs-Elysées, led out by his team-mate Bradley Wiggins in the yellow jersey. That milestone Tour triumph came together in just three years, and for the team now to have done it twice – and to witness Chris Froome standing on the podium in the centenary edition alongside five-times winners Eddy Merckx, Bernard Hinault and Miguel Indurain – is amazing.

There is a deep sense of community among the Team Sky outfit. As a team we worked on a very refined model in 2012, bound by our philosophy. This year we tried to scale that up and have a broader service provision so that we could have a good go at the other Grand Tours – the Giro d'Italia and the Vuelta a España. Before the season starts you look at 27 riders. Each Grand Tour only needs nine riders. The trick is to optimise resources against the goals we've set. Bradley's goal for 2013 was to win the Giro. Chris's sole objective was the Tour de France. You make plans a long way out and sometimes life gets in the way, but we put in a dynamic framework that allows us to amend plans if necessary.

We went to the Giro with pre-race speculation bubbling about whether it would be Vincenzo Nibali or Bradley first or second in Brescia. After Bradley's unfortunate withdrawal through illness, we still achieved second on the podium with Plan B and Rigoberto Urán, which was a terrific result. You could see the team's trademark action during the epic stage that Rigoberto won, when we used strength in numbers to go on the attack and execute a pre-planned move. The lads worked hard and Rigoberto went at exactly the right time, gaining a chunk of time with his first GT stage win in Altopiano del Montasio. We took away a lot of positives from our quest for the *maglia rosa*.

The 100th edition of the Tour de France meant it was a symbolic race. It was also the first since the Lance Armstrong revelations. It's a strange situation: the sport is cleaner now than ever but, because of the revelations of past riders, it's getting closer scrutiny and the current riders are having to take this because of the misdemeanours of the past. Reporters have a duty to ask the questions, but they also set the tone. Riders are smart enough to understand why they're being asked, but it still doesn't make it easy.

Otherwise, going into the Tour felt similar in many respects to last year: Chris's brilliant run-up replicated the wins achieved by Bradley in 2012. Chris, too, hit the race as pre-Tour favourite. Instead of thinking it was our title to defend, which would have been a negative mindset, we went out to try and win it a second time starting from zero. That gave us a more positive way of looking at it. Bradley, the reigning champion, was unable to compete; Chris was coming up through the ranks, very hungry, very driven.

Chris had been second in the Vuelta in 2011, second in the Tour in 2012. Having set his sights on winning the 2013 Tour, he demonstrated an amazing growth in self-belief. He concentrated on learning how to be a race and team leader. He put himself in situations against the best riders in the world and he wasn't afraid to take them on. When you're riding to support a leader who can take it on, it's a great cause. The team had difficult days, yet Chris stayed absolutely calm. He'd say, 'No worries, we're in control.' The art of leadership is not to show anxiety or concern, but to do what it takes to achieve your goal. Chris proved he was the best bike rider in the race. No issue.

INTRODUCTION BY DAVE BRAILSFORD

THE STORY OF THE GIRO

STAGE 1 / p.12

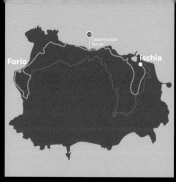

STAGE 2 / p.16

STAGE 3 / p.18

STAGE 7 / p.34

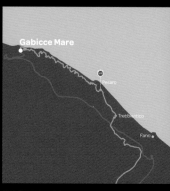

STAGE 8 / p.40

STAGE 9 / p.44

STAGE 13 / p.58

STAGE 14 / p.62

STAGE 15 / p.68

THE GIRO ROUTE

STAGE 4 / p.24

STAGE 5 / p.26

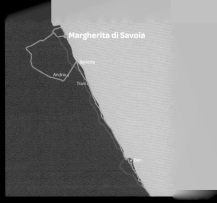

STAGE 6 / p.32

STAGE 10 / p.48

STAGE 11 / p.54

STAGE 12 / p.56

STAGE 16 / p.74

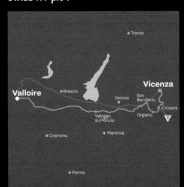

STAGE 17 / p.76

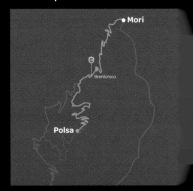

STAGE 18 / p.78

The Giro d'Italia. *La Corsa Rosa*. The toughest Grand Tour of them all. Never mind its bubble-gum branding, the Italian job is the Tour de France's monster brother. The crazy one. A race that serves up brutal climbs, perilous descents, fraught finishes, extremes of weather, depths of anguish. And on Saturday 4 May 2013 – under azure skies, with Mount Vesuvius looming portentously in the background – it was *Grande Partenza* time, the moment the clock starts ticking and the contest begins.

Over the course of 21 days of relentless race and recovery, one individual from the throng of 207 tautly primed riders rolling out on the Naples seafront would arrive at the finish in Brescia, a tired body but elated spirit, having pedalled himself into cycling's history books.

The *Grande Partenza* was also the start of the tale of what Sir Bradley Wiggins did next. Shorn of hair and trademark sideburns, the Team Sky leader was in combat mode as he prepared to take on the nerve-inducing jostle of fresh riders, the responsibility of never having a bad day, and embark on three weeks that could cement his place among the greats. Looking to follow up his Tour de France and Olympic triumphs of 2012, he had set his sights on becoming the first Briton to win the famed *maglia rosa*. The experience of claiming the yellow jersey and a gold medal within ten magical days was unsurpassable, but Wiggins still had unfinished business. The Giro held a 'love–hate' appeal for him. Fuelled by childhood memories

STAGE 1

of the heroics of Miguel Indurain on VHS and by his own thwarted attempts (elimination in 2003, early crashes in 2010), the goal was to add the Giro to his unparalleled *palmarès*.

'The Giro has always been a race I'd love to win,' he said, before the nine-strong squads from 23 teams gathered to sign in. The daunting stretches he'd ridden in preparation prompted a doleful afterthought. 'There have been times, even though I'm physically in great shape, when I think, "Why on earth did I choose to do this bloody race?"'

The annual quest for the *maglia rosa* is the stuff of legends. Beyond the business of staying on the bike in the hurly-burly of racing full gas over Italy's challenging terrain, the Giro also comes laced with gruelling transfers, narrow roads, an air of potential chaos. 'I was super-nervous,' said Dan Hunt, one of Team Sky's sports directors. 'You're walking into the unknown. You don't know how it will pan out. For me, the first week was the equal of the Olympics in terms of external pressure, because Brad was going out to win the Giro. It's one thing to compete in a Grand Tour. It's

difficult going in to win. The world wanted to see if Brad and Team Sky could achieve it.'

With Wiggins anticipating 'the usual carnage', he began his assault confident in the team around him. The Colombian climbing specialists Rigoberto Urán and Sergio Henao (who came seventh and ninth respectively in the 2011 Giro) would provide support in the mountains. Christian Knees of Germany was road captain; the versatile Kanstantsin Siutsou of Belarussia a trusted lieutenant. Danny Pate of the United States added an experienced understanding of peloton dynamics. Xabier Zandio of Spain contributed a powerful engine and a big heart. The Italian duo of Dario Cataldo, national time trial champion, and the youngster Salvatore Puccio, would generate a buzz in their home race.

Nearly three hours after passing kilometre zero, the tight and twisty 156km opener served up a fierce sprint finale and a slingshot winner in Mark Cavendish. Team Sky emerged intact. 'It was a bit hairy, as expected, but we made it through,' said Wiggins. One down, 20 to go.

A team time trial requires a series of short, intense efforts as riders take turns at the front of their train. This one, hosted by the island of Ischia, also called for strong stomachs. It would be an early wake-up call and a long day for the riders and attendant Giro circus because of the need to sail by ferry to Ischia and then back to Sorrento on the mainland, south of Naples, ready for the next day's road stage to Marina di Ascea.

'The team time trial is known as the worst day on a Grand Tour because it's hectic, nervy and very, very stressful. A lot more can go wrong than go right. It was going to be 17.4km right on the rivet,' said Hunt, who was bringing his clinical approach as former head of the GB men's team pursuit squad to this choreographed race feature.

Rigoberto Urán concurred. 'Team time trials are very complicated in the management of different people's strengths,' he said. 'We've a mixture of climbers, workers and time trial specialists. Bradley is so strong; he was going to do a lot of the work, but get the distribution of effort wrong and it can be painful. If you're not 100 per cent, it's agony, because you're at full gas the whole distance. But we managed that well . . . and that's why we won.'

Wiggins, Urán, Cataldo, Henao and Puccio crossed the line together in a time of 22 minutes and 5 seconds, set up brilliantly by turns from Pate, Knees, Siutsou and Zandio. The victory established a 9 seconds margin over Movistar and 14 seconds over Vincenzo Nibali's Astana. 'It was a big highlight, really cool to be part of that,' said Pate. 'Puccio in the pink jersey! He was over the moon – and he's a very stereotypical Italian!'

As if proof of the Giro's inherent unpredictability, it was young Salvatore Puccio – not Dario Cataldo, Team Sky's Italian national time trial champion – who was awarded the *maglia rosa*. 'There was confusion because Dario was the first rider across the line but Puccio was the leading Team Sky rider after the first stage,' said Knees. 'Dario had been sent to wait by the stage for the podium ceremony. Salvatore was in the shower when I heard the commentator confirm the results. I had to knock on the shower and tell Puccio he'd won the jersey. He was saying, "No, no, no, it must be Dario," and I was yelling, "No, it's you, quick, get out of the shower!"'

STAGE 2

'Salvatore was absolutely flummoxed. He, we, didn't
expect it,' says Hunt. 'Sky had never won a team time trial
in a Grand Tour before, so it was a first, a great day for the
team. To see Salvatore in pink was the icing on the cake.'

After the podium ceremony, Puccio fulfilled his
media obligations, including an extensive interview with
La Gazzetta dello Sport. Accompanied by team doctor
Richard Freeman, he then had to report to doping control
and missed the ferry back to the mainland. 'The organisers
had a speedboat ready to take him to Sorrento,' laughs
Hunt. 'The doc lived it up, lounging on the back of the boat
like a playboy, but Puccio was seasick!'

STAGE 3

Morale was high for the first foray into medium mountains with Team Sky's Giro débutant still incredulous that he would be the one wearing the iconic *maglia rosa*. Puccio had gone to sleep with the jersey on the seat next to his bed, pinned up with his race numbers ready for the next stage. At the morning meeting in a hotel bedroom, he was the only one not wearing a jersey. The pink pile of fabric remained bundled by his side until the others left the room and he enjoyed the private moment of pulling it on over his head, tweaking the fit and admiring himself in the mirror. Downstairs in the lobby, his father, girlfriend and best friends were waiting to surprise him; they had set off at 4am and driven six hours to make his day even more special. 'It is a great honour to wear the *maglia rosa*,' he said. 'As this is my first experience in the Giro, it took time to understand all this was reality and not a dream.'

'It was a nice day for "Baby Puccio",' said Knees. 'The *Gazzetta dello Sport* called him that in their report and I took it up and ran with it. He hadn't dreamed he'd be in pink, and now he had a pink helmet, pink saddle and pink grip on his handle bars!' The *tifosi* in Sorrento town centre were buzzing. In a race that boasted a strong international field, the race leader's jersey was on the back of an Italian for the first time in 2013. Standing out in that distinctive pink – even above the assembled mass of dayglo team kits and helmets – Puccio was loving every minute of the experience, receiving congratulations from riders, fielding banter from fellow Italians, waiting under the rose-tinged shade provided by an official umbrella girl for the signal to roll off. The great thing for Wiggins and the GC contenders – Nibali, Cadel Evans and defending champion Ryder Hesjedal – was that the home media had an alternative focus away from the intense speculation about their rivalry and form.

Looking at the course, analysing its demands and assessing the attributes required for a serious campaign are an exercise all the teams undertake as soon as the race route is published. The 2013 Giro d'Italia had its traditional quotient of massive mountains – 'They tend to find new super-steep climbs each year,' notes senior sports director Marcus Ljungqvist – but it also had a fair amount of time trialling. This would normally play into the hands of Wiggins, but Nibali, third behind Wiggins and Chris Froome in the 2012 Tour de France, was super-motivated to take the challenge to the British knight.

Riding on home soil, for a new team, Astana – which had built itself around its lead rider's ambitions – Nibali had worked doggedly at improving his time-trialling performance so that he could consolidate the advantages

his steely descending prowess would doubtless win him. He arrived in Naples on tremendous form, having won the Tirreno–Adriatico (holding off Froome in the final time trial) and the Giro del Trentino, and had sent the odd psychological salvo in Wiggins's direction. There was no doubt he meant business.

Cadel Evans, ultra-competitive in spirit but recovering from a virus, came in with only five weeks of dedicated training compared with other contenders' six months or so and admitted his entry was 'a bit of an experiment'. Race form was also a question mark over Ryder Hesjedal, as was the amount of time trialling (not his speciality) in this edition of the Giro. Samuel Sánchez's legendary appetite for courageous descending put him in the mix even at the age of 35. But pre-Tour speculation evaporated in the edginess of the third day. The Giro had not yet developed a rhythm. Teams had not shown their cards. It wasn't clear who had good legs. It was all about the here and now, with everyone trying to stay safe.

An early seven-man breakaway led the peloton by more than 6 minutes when Team Sky, Katusha and Omega Pharma-Quick Step took turns to up the tempo at the front. Wiggins, Nibali and Hesjedal were visible in the lead group. Hesjedal twice attacked, but happily slotted back into the pack, before Luca Paolini – leaving the big guns to stalk and unnerve each other with surprise bursts and dummy moves – escaped with a late attack on the descent.

It was a day bookended by two Italian Giro debutants in pink as Baby Puccio surrendered the jersey to his compatriot, 36-year-old Paolini. 'We knew there would be a lot of teams going for it at the end and that's how it played out,' said Ljungqvist. 'It was always going to be a tough finale. We set a tempo at the front, and Xabi and Danny did a great job to control things there with the breakaway up the road. Today was really nice for Puccio but now we're back to looking after Brad and making sure we're ready for the hard days coming up.'

The Giro always throws in a couple of hard stages early on, and the 246km stage from Policastro Bussentino down the Mediterranean coast to Serra San Bruno was a trademark shocker. As legs were beginning to long for the masseur's attention on the second-longest stage of the race, up loomed the Category-3 climb of Vibo Valentia, followed by the Category-2 challenge of Croce Ferrata and a 7km downhill run to a finish on cobbles. 'The Giro finishes are always a bit more technical,' warned team principal Sir Dave Brailsford. 'You have to be on your guard, focused and concentrated, ready for any attack at any time.'

Braced for more than six hours of racing, for over-excited breakaways and for probing GC moves, Team Sky put on a dominant display of teamwork, particularly on the climb up Croce Ferrata and the hazardous descent to the finish. 'We've our own style of racing,' said Knees. 'As we're strong throughout the team, we make races hard tempo so everyone has to fight to stay on our wheel. We pull at such a pace that only very few can follow us. The Giro is always a bit different. It's more chaotic, harder to control. The plan was to get Bradley in pink – any moment would be fine, we didn't target a stage – and defend the lead. Then life becomes easier. Taking control of a race is what we're good at. Fighting to get control of a race is more difficult.'

Going into battle with Knees as bodyguard and road captain could be classed as one of Team Sky's famous 'marginal gains'. The German – who at 1.94m is unusually tall for a professional cyclist – first rode in support of Wiggins in the 2011 Tour de France. Since then, he has been a key *domestique* on the flat and in low mountains, a hugely effective windshield and periscope in the peloton. 'My role is to stay around him [Wiggins] and look out for potential problems. He's the man who needs to conserve energy. If he sees a hole and moves up, I can expend energy to come up ahead of him to protect him from the wind. He gets a good slipstream behind me. And because I'm so tall,

I have a great race overview. It's a big plus for me and my team. I can see how the bunch is moving. I can see before anyone else if there's a left or right turn coming. I can assess what the others are doing and weigh up the risks to ensure Bradley stays safe.'

The most demoralising scenario, of course, is when a long spell of hard work is ruined by a moment of bad luck. As the sun disappeared, grey clouds descended and damp fog shrouded the route up Vibo Valentia. Nibali had put on a little look-at-me show of descending bravura, but all was on track. Wiggins, led by Urán, Henao and Siutsou at a pace that had riders falling off the back of the group, was well placed. Could this be the day he went into pink?

But no, the last 20 minutes erupted into all sorts of drama on the descent. A crash involving Cristiano Salerno of Italy on the approach to the final stretch held up the Team Sky leader. Confusion reigned. The 3km rule – which states that riders caught up in such incidents within that distance of the finish line are not penalised – was not applied. The race jury decided that Wiggins had already been gapped in the final run-in and was not hindered by the crash. As a result, he fell from second to sixth in the general classification, 34 seconds behind race leader Paolini. 'You can gain hard-earned seconds here and there, and then you can lose time very quickly,' said Brailsford, after confirmation of the results. 'Ultimately, this first week's all about staying in contention. This race will be won and lost in the time trials and the high mountains. Bradley's in great shape, mentally and physically.'

Urán, who moved to second overall behind Paolini, added a further positive perspective. 'Second for me doesn't mean anything. Bradley and the GC guys are all up there. Long-term, it makes no difference. I'm not thinking about my position. I've other things on my mind – to work for Bradley. It's a long race.'

STAGE 4

STAGE 5

Another day, another dramatic crash on the final run-in – this time caused by Luka Mezgec of Slovenia, who skidded across a slippery left-hander in the final kilometre – but Wiggins emerged unscathed and without loss of time. That was a relief at the end of a stressful day for the *directeurs sportifs*. All the teams had a similar game plan – to be towards the front going over the top of the first big climb. 'We went full-gas up it for our GC guys,' said Dario Cataldo, who was recovering from a severe stomach bug. 'Luckily the descent that followed was dry, because it had been raining heavily before we arrived. Unfortunately Rigo punctured soon afterwards . . .'

Danny Pate took up the story: 'That was a chaotic moment. We were going really fast. Sometimes directions are hard to take over the radio when you're riding as hard as you can. The message was they didn't know where Rigo was. So, I have to go from focusing on the role I'm

concentrating on, to trying to find Rigo. I kept rolling . . . He appeared . . . And we both take our front wheels, but they won't come out quick-release. I've never had that experience before! We're smashing our wheels, and it was sorted pretty quick. Rigo was on and I gave him a push. The two Italian guys helped him back. That was my day over; I could take it easy to the end.'

The effort to get Urán back in the pack was exhausting, but Cataldo, Puccio and Zandio managed it 100m before that last ascent. Afterwards, Ljungqvist was quick to praise Cataldo's stalwart efforts. 'He's done well to battle through his illness and hopefully now he's coming out the other side.'

According to the team doctor, Richard Freeman, Cataldo picked up an infection early in the race. 'It's not unusual. When they're training hard the immune system is diminished. The first week is actually the time riders are most likely to get sick. Training culminates, and tapers. Travel to the Grand Tours has its risks. They're mixing with the general public, meeting people from all over the world. Dario was gutted. After months of training, it's bad enough to fall off your bike – but to go down with a common-or-garden infection is frustrating. Because of the nature of the Giro, it was hard to get on top of his bug. Every day he was exhausting himself, four, five, six hours in the saddle. He was isolated and given his own room. The chef made special food, which I took up to him on a tray. He liked it so much that at 2.30am he called me, wanting more!'

Rain, punctures, crashes, illness . . . The sunny times on Ischia seemed a world away. 'For sure, it happens every Grand Tour,' said Dan Hunt, cheerfully. 'There isn't a team that doesn't go through adversity. It's a "here we go" sort of thing. That's the kind of sport it is. Illness takes the edge off you, but you tend to get through it in a couple of days. We do express sympathy, but the guys are pretty brutal with each other. There's a lot of banter and taking the piss.'

STAGE 6

'Our goal will be to keep Bradley, Rigo and Sergio out of trouble and allow the other guys, like Dario, to rest up as much as possible before the tough test tomorrow.' So declared Marcus Ljungqvist on the morning of a day on which the sprinters' teams were expected to control things from start to finish. It was a sound idea but, as usual, Lady Luck had other plans. The route hugged the picturesque Adriatic coastline before arriving in Margherita di Savoia, where two laps of the 16.6km Circuito Delle Saline saw the sprinters move into their most maniacal form of queue-barging just as space became tight, making crashes inevitable.

Wiggins, who famously hates the first week of a Grand Tour, had yet another early scare on a fourth consecutive nerve-shredding day. First, he suffered a mechanical problem that forced a bike change. Just as he was settling back at pace, in position on the first of the two laps of the finishing circuit, he found himself barricaded behind a crash and an extensive tangle of bikes, spinning wheels and ripped Lycra. Aided by his team-mates, he managed to hitch back on to the leading group – which had slowed by convention, albeit somewhat reluctantly – and remarkably ended up leading the pack with 3km remaining.

It was an admirable show of resilience, but for road captain Knees it was an equally fretful experience. 'Bradley needed a bike change minutes before that crash, so although he wasn't involved in it, he did get stuck behind it,' the German confirmed. 'The boys did a brilliant job pacing him back on, but I got caught up the road. It was so loud in the bunch that I couldn't hear over the race radio what had happened behind me until it was too late. When I found out, I went straight to the front and told the FDJ and Quick Step guys to stop pulling. They agreed to ease off a little, but the pace was still high, so the boys had to ride hard to bring Bradley back on. They did a great job, and I then moved him towards the front to keep him out of any further trouble. This was the last sprint day for a while, so that's why it was so hectic. We knew we had to stay safe at the front. In the end we did that, so we're all happy with how things turned out.'

Wiggins was relieved to tick off another stage with his overall title hopes intact. He was one of the first to congratulate former Sky team-mate Mark Cavendish, who – at last – had enjoyed a textbook lead-out from his new team, Omega Pharma-Quick Step. Cav went on to dedicate his win to the memory of Belgian rider Wouter Weylandt, who had crashed and died exactly two years ago to the day.

Ljungqvist was left relieved, if a tad rueful, about the difference a few hours can make to his day-by-day Giro overview. 'That was a fantastic team performance today and everything worked out in the end. As soon as Bradley needed a new bike, there were seven riders around him and Christian was able to slow things down up the road. It took some hard work to bring Bradley back on, but these guys will recover tonight ahead of a tough day tomorrow.'

There is no such sentiment as 'Thank God it's Friday' in the professional cyclist's week. Nothing about the profile (a continuously testing route, marked by four tricky categorised climbs and an irritating series of small, steep ramps) or the conditions (heavy downpours and greasy roads) suggested that Friday 10 May would include a happy hour. The forecast had always been 'tough'; the reality for Team Sky was worse. Every day, Brailsford had gee'ed up Wiggins by exhorting him to count down the days until Saturday's individual time trial. 'Get through today with concentration,' he'd say from the rear of the team bus during the *directeurs sportifs*' presentation of the day's stage profile. 'It's another day gone, another box ticked.' On paper, this was the last of those days that had to be survived.

The Giro seemed now to be travelling in its own microclimate of glowering skies and perpetual rain. However long the transfer between stages, whatever the bearing – eastwards, northwards, north-westwards – the team always stepped off the bus to find the weather had not brightened. 'When it's raining, I don't love it,' said Wiggins glumly. On that Friday ride into Pescara, the conditions were testing and the pace fast. The peloton went through its usual dynamic at accelerated speed – the riders settling into the stage, marshalling potential breakaways and eventually releasing a small group that wouldn't threaten anyone's specific ambitions – and then started to splinter dramatically under the lashing rain and the demands of the sharply undulating route.

'It was a complicated day. The weather was very cold, the conditions were very difficult, we were going full-gas from the start,' said Urán. 'It was a fast day, uphill, very hard, attacking on climb after climb because of the pressure other teams were putting on Bradley. Both Sergio and I were working hard for Bradley to bring him back on to the lead group after each attack. We were leading him out. I was calm. I had no worries. And then Bradley fell.'

Wiggins was one of many, including race leader Paolini, who slid and fell as they powered downhill at high speed. His tumble came as he attempted to round one of the mountain hairpins on the final descent. 'Sergio and I were waiting around the next corner for him, but he didn't come,' Urán continues. 'Usually he gets straight back up, but when he didn't appear we started to wonder if he'd broken his collarbone. Eventually he came back, but his head was not fully there. It was pissing down. It was cold. He was knackered. We tried to guide him back to the front to make up the time, but he'd lost his concentration.'

The Team Sky leader rode gingerly to the line – right elbow and knee bloodied, his ripped Lycra also revealing a grazed hip – to discover he had dropped from sixth place to 23rd, and had lost 1 minute and 24 seconds to all his major rivals.

'It's all about how much balls Brad has now,' was how Brailsford put in to the media, as he consigned the day to the ticked-off list and pointed to the recovery potential offered by the next day's individual time trial. Once earmarked as the stage on which Wiggins could unleash his natural prowess against the clock and launch himself into the high mountains with a comfortable lead over his rivals, the 'Race of Truth' was now another ultra-stressful day, a pivotal day of catch-up.

How serious were his injuries? Would they affect him going forward? 'Bradley's crash was not anything

STAGE 7

spectacular and would have had negligible effect on performance,' said team doc Richard Freeman, who was following in the team car. 'A graze is painful and uncomfortable. He lost skin on his hip, elbow and knee, but it wouldn't have stopped him performing. Grazes are a normal issue. There was no deep tissue damage. It would have been worse if there had been a bleed into the muscle or a bruised bone. But if you're already miserable, those kind of injuries make you even more miserable . . .'

Hmm. For the first time, observers started to wonder if there was something else gnawing at Wiggins beyond the first-week trials and tribulations. Vincenzo Nibali had also had a fall on the same descent, but had bounced back up and pressed on like a man possessed, to rejoin the group that vainly chased the day's breakaway winner, Adam Hansen. Wiggins seemed a tiny percentage off his characteristic form. How much was he out of sorts?

'Not much seemed out of the ordinary to us,' said Danny Pate. 'Those days are still kind of normal for the Giro. But Brad really compartmentalises his own emotions. He may have seen the storm coming. He was feeling bad in his own health and he was really not enjoying those bad-weather days. But he was getting through them. One thing a team leader doesn't do is be super-negative and drag down the team. Brad's best quality is that he doesn't do that. We never knew until much later that he was starting to feel ill.'

Urán and Henao also plummeted out of the top ten – Urán was down to 22nd, when he might have been in the *maglia rosa* had he not turned back for his leader. Typically, he was not bothered. 'I do what the team asks me to do, whether I'm working for a team leader or I'm leading myself. It might have put me in a good position if I hadn't had to stop, but my job is to wait for my team leader.' But with that sense that the team leader was not descending well, the outside world questioned the team principal on the decision to send the Colombians back. 'It's the team's call,' said Brailsford. 'Urán and Henao are here to ride for a leader. When you're dedicated to a single leader, that's the call that the team makes and that's the right call as far as I'm concerned. You've got to take setbacks on the chin and you have to show character. That's what it's all about. You have to keep fighting right until the end and that's what we'll aim to do.

'There's a long way to go. Bradley's fine. There's no physical injury. Ultimately, when you have difficult conditions like these and hard racing, this type of thing can happen. It's the Giro. You can have good days and bad days, and you have to wait until the end to tot them all up and see where you are. It's a setback, but Brad's still very much in the hunt. We've now got to take each day as it comes, focus on fully recovering tonight and hitting the time trial hard tomorrow. We'll see where we are tomorrow night, and take stock of the situation then.'

STAGE 8

The pivotal day dawned. Could Wiggins do his stuff and claim the *maglia rosa*? Waiting for each rider, rolling down the start ramp at two-minute intervals, was a 54.8km course that challenged technical skill as much as stamina and judgement of pace. The fan-lined ramp up to the finish at Saltara was a sting in the tail, giving spectators a close-up view of the agony etched on each rider's face as they eked out their last watt of power towards the line. As Wiggins noted, 'It's one of those tests where you have to be good from start to finish. If you die off at the end, you're going to lose three minutes on the final climb.'

Team Sky approached the potential Sir Bradley Wiggins masterclass with customary forensic scrutiny. Wiggins had ridden the route, studied videos and absorbed the opinions of his support team. The plan was to get up early, ride the first 30km again, drive the final 25km, then get on the turbo bike, plug in the pump-up music and let the adrenalin take over.

Under cloudy skies and sporadic sunshine, Alex Dowsett – a former Team Sky rider and Giro débutant – set a time early on that was proving unmatchable for rider after ever more highly placed rider. As Wiggins sped off the starting gantry, alone in a private world of pain and focus, his junior compatriot's time of 1 hour, 16 minutes and 27 seconds was still the time to beat. Wiggins was the Olympic road time trial champion, an undisputed expert at getting from A to B with superb aerodynamic efficiency, but it was nerve-wracking watching his progress over the tight, technical course. The winding narrow country lanes made it difficult to get into a rhythm. The previous day had not been an ideal lead-in, but surely here he could reverse the momentum of the last week for himself?

Eighteen minutes in – yet more wretched luck. Wiggins was indicating 'puncture' with a frantic gesture to the team car shadowing him. He was off his new Pinarello Bolide time trial bike, chucking it into the hedge, and back on his old Graal model, trying to stay in the zone, striving to re-establish his rhythm. It was another blow. The loss of precious seconds left him 'a bit ruffled'. At the first intermediate split, he was 52 seconds down, only seventh fastest.

'We did a swift bike swap but he lost advantage there and broke his rhythm,' said Dan Hunt, who was in radio contact with him from the car behind. 'I started to get this feeling . . . There are problems everywhere we turn.'

Digging in deep, Wiggins made up time in the latter part of the course and finished second, 10 seconds down on Dowsett. It was a result that left him not in the pink jersey – and not with a sizeable cushion of a lead to defend in the mountains – but in fourth place overall, 1 minute and 16 seconds down on Nibali, and behind Cadel Evans and the Dutchman Robert Gesink. 'It's all to play for, still,' he said phlegmatically. 'There was initial disappointment because I wanted to win the stage. But it is what it is. It's going to be a hell of a race for the next two weeks.'

It was another thrilling day of unpredictable action and unsung heroes – and yet more skid-pan corners, as leaden skies dropped relentless waves of heavy rain. While Maxim Belkov of Russia broke clear of a breakaway on the penultimate climb, the Vallombrosa, soloing his way to a 44-second clear victory, the peloton was hyperactive with all sorts of attacks and probing moves. 'It wasn't super pleasant out there,' said Danny Pate. 'It was fast from the start. A couple of different groups formed and then finally we got the breakaway. It was quite big, and having one guy in there – Juan Manuel Gárate, who was only 5 minutes down in the GC – the peloton never let it go out very far.

'The two big climbs in the middle were hard, too. When it was time to bridge the gap we stayed together. Any time you have to do a chase, one of the key things is not to panic. We tried to bring our group back to the main group and we managed it right on the Category-3 climb. We had Rigo and Sergio ahead, and everyone else was behind helping Brad. After he got back on, that was it – I was pretty much blown!'

All eyes were on Wiggins, who had dropped back on the long series of bends off the same mountain Belkov used as his launch pad to victory. Although his team-mates escorted him at pace for 20km to regain contact with the *maglia rosa* group, questions were arising about whether the British knight had lost his 'descending mojo'. The toil required to rejoin the group demanded an enormous effort from Wiggins, too. Although he had his Team Sky colleagues to help, he did much of the work himself, leaving himself empty as he struggled to hold on during the day's final two climbs, shorter and punchier than those that had preceded them, and looked in peril again on the descent from Fiesole.

'I was riding right behind him,' said Giovanni Visconti. 'I could see he was handling the descents very badly. I think when it comes to descents he's now got some kind of mental block.' You could dismiss that as a bit of psychological warfare from another team, but Christian Knees made a similar observation: 'Bradley was a little bit nervous downhill. Bad luck with the weather meant the roads were very slippery. He still had confidence in his climbing skills and his ability. He kept fighting. He was the same Bradley, mentally thinking all the time about how to win, but he was a little bit cautious.' Two days later, Wiggins, never one to make excuses, reflected on his performance and said: 'Let's be honest. I descended like a bit of a girl after the crash . . . Not to disrespect girls, I have

one at home. But that's life and we have to push on and deal with the disappointments.'

'Everyone thinks uphill is the big challenge, but downhill can play a big part,' said Pate. 'Uphill, you need a good power-to-weight ratio. Downhill, you need to be a bit crazy. Some descents are over 100 km/h. They're fun, exhilarating, scary, frightening . . . how you take them all depends on who you are. Some guys have way more confidence than skill and ability. Some guys are out of their minds. People think the sprinters are crazy. Some of the downhill guys are crazy, too. Personally, I'm okay downhill, but if I crash it definitely takes me back a notch. It takes me a while to regain confidence. You can get really shaken up – but some guys don't get shaken up; a crash doesn't affect them.

'The Giro is an annual race, but every edition has different stages, routes, climbs and descents,' he continues. 'Some descents are fast, some are more technical, with tight turns. It's a real mix, all on one road. I think the Giro is unique in that aspect. A lot of road we're riding pretty blind. We have profiles, radio information, maps, but there's always going to be stuff we haven't raced down. It can be pretty tricky. To my mind, there's risk and there's reward, but some guys are definitely big risk-takers. Nibali is known for being good at going downhill, but I've seen him crash quite a bit. He crashed twice that same day Brad did, but he doesn't get shaken up. A guy crashed at the same time, just behind Nibali, and he broke ribs, a scapula and collarbone. That could have been Nibali – out of the Giro, and all for an unnecessary downhill attack.'

Tellingly, Nibali told Italian TV station RAI afterwards that he had not been exploiting the difficulties Wiggins was encountering because he was unaware of them. His team car had been relegated to last position after a previous rule infraction. By the time BMC and Garmin-Sharp had moved to the front to try and force the pace, Wiggins and Team Sky were already bridging back across.

So, Wiggins remained in fourth going into the rest day. The day's big loser was Ryder Hesjedal, who lost more than a minute to his rivals and slipped out of the top ten after being dropped on the final climb. 'The stage worked out well in the end for us,' said Ljungqvist. 'The guys raced as a team, didn't panic and that was the key. We were able to chase down the gap and we've moved up the GC with Rigoberto and Sergio. We have to be happy with that after a hard stage like this.'

STAGE 9

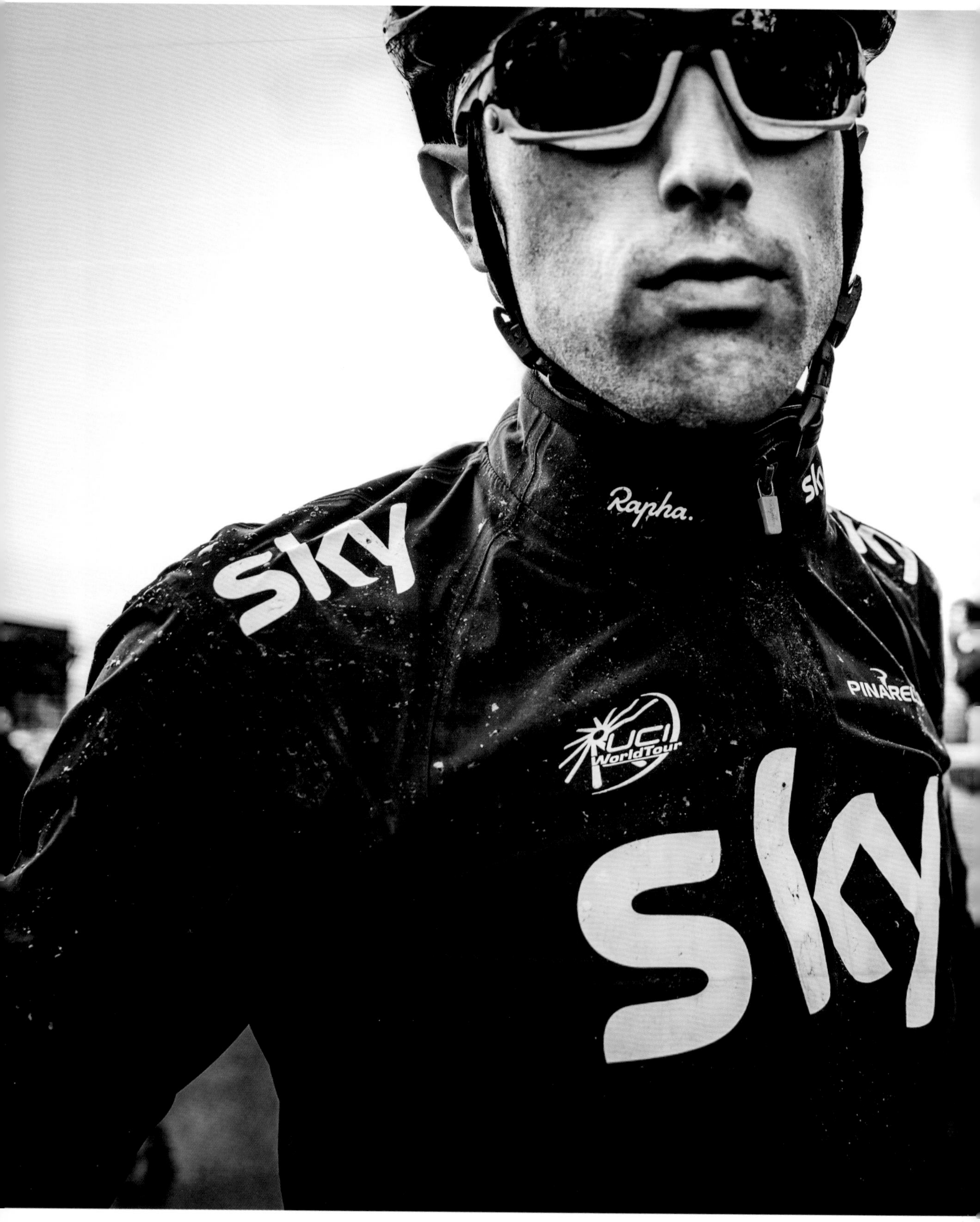
sky
Rapha.
UCI
WorldTour
sky

The race moved to the high mountains of north-east Italy to deliver the first summit finish. The climb to Altopiano del Montasio was new to the Giro – one of those super-steep peaks that Ljungqvist jokes the organisers manage to discover each year – and posed one of the hardest finishes in the race. At the toughest part of the ascent, which lasts about a kilometre, the gradient registered 20 per cent. It was a key stage, the day when the big GC contenders came up against the climbers, with a major reshuffle expected in the overall standings.

This is where Team Sky's Colombian riders – Rigoberto Urán and Sergio Henao – come into their element. Both have superb all-round qualities, but explosive climbing is their speciality. While most professional cyclists spend short periods in altitude training camps (where the body adapts to the relative lack of oxygen by increasing the mass of red blood cells that oxygenate the body), many Colombians have a natural physiological advantage as a result of their country's topography.

STAGE 10

It was no surprise that it was a Colombian 1–2 on the podium at the end of the day, after a stunning solo victory from Urán, who powered off from 8km to go, without getting out of the saddle. Wiggins, meanwhile, saw his team-mate off, but lost touch as the gradient ramped up in that final stretch. He maintained fourth place overall, 1 second behind Urán, losing further time to Nibali.

'I love the mountains, particularly when I look around on a climb and see how much the other riders are suffering!' said Urán. 'Every rider is picked with his own job to do. We all know what our job is and once we have done it we drop back at certain pre-planned points. On a high-mountain stage, once the group is down to the 30 best riders, the pain starts and then I attack. I have other attributes, but I really love climbing.'

'In the morning meeting it was Brad's idea to be aggressive with Rigo, and Brad would follow,' said Danny Pate. 'We would ride the Sky way, on the forefront, and everyone would just pack up. The plan was to be aggressive and, I guess, progressive. You want to have your own plan and execute it.'

'It was an incredible day, the teamwork was strong and we rode hard all day to put pressure on other teams,' said Urán. 'The plan was for me to attack at 7 to 8km out. Looking at the stage profile card, I knew that meant 30 minutes of effort, giving my maximum at gradient, right on the limit. I knew if I scaled my effort according to the distance, I could win. Over the radio, they were telling me the finish line was close, but when you hear that, it somehow stretches out! You feel you're never going to reach it. When I actually saw the finish, I felt energy flood through me, even though I was riding off the scale. It was an unforgettable moment. After three Grand Tours, it was a massive thing to win my first stage, an emotional day for me – and for the team, after all the expectations on Bradley and the problems we were encountering. To pull off that win was a special moment.'

'Rigo's win was a huge boost,' said Pate. 'You finish a tough day with a result like that and it makes you look forward to the next one. If you remember you won on the last hard day, you almost start to look forward to them.'

The day began slowly courtesy of an armistice in the peloton. The previous day's exertions called for a collective decision to ride a gentle first 60km. Riders enjoyed an easy warm-up before a walloping 120-odd kilometres over the mountains to Erto e Casso. Harried *directeurs sportifs*, following in team cars, also had a welcome respite from being in 'red alert' mode, ever-poised to assess the race pattern through swishing windscreen wipers, to deliver crucial information over radios that don't always work in mountains and rainstorms, and to offer tactical support as the daily peloton fireworks exploded.

'*DS*-ing the Giro, I think, is the hardest job in the world. It's so chaotic and stressful,' says Dan Hunt. 'Marcus, the senior directeur sportif, was doing a great job in very hard scenarios. As it turned out, very few more things could have gone wrong than did in this year's Giro.'

The fundamental responsibility for everyone lay in ensuring Bradley Wiggins got from Naples to Brescia, safely, healthily, more quickly than his rivals. Wiggins was supported, not just by his eight colleagues in the saddle, but by a Team Sky staff of 22, a roll-call that included *directeurs sportifs*, performance staff, doctor, physiotherapist, carers, mechanics, chef, press officers and bus driver. All play a crucial role around the clock, but during a race it's the riders and *directeur sportif* alone in a bubble of competitive survival. Riders have a manual for the race, but on a bike they can't access that or glance at a map. They're in a high-pressure environment – the argy-bargy of the peloton – so it's vital to receive info over race radio about wind speed or direction, cautions about crosswinds or crashes, wet patches on the road or emergency vehicles, and to receive a countdown of the distance to the start of a big climb so that the team can position itself.

'The car is there for back-up, with a mechanic and the doc, but often we see what's going on, or we know where Bradley is, before race radio,' says Danny Pate. 'The dynamic inside a race is a weird thing and it's different each day dependent on how the overall standings are looking. There's a bigger mind-set on any given day depending on who's on what time, who's going for the mountain jersey, the sprint points, the young rider category, who's in a breakaway, who's got personal vendettas. Each of these scenarios could play a big role in each day's action. You have to be aware of these, plus the tactical problems too. Your GC contender can't ride with the top ten guys on the road all the time. You have to be attentive. If a group goes away and there's someone dangerous in there, you might have to chase it back. You have to stay on top of all that stuff. It can be complicated.'

STAGE 11

It could have been a gentle few hours on the flat while the sprinters eyed up their chances on this shortest stage of the race, but the journey to Tarvisio was another sodden, wind-buffeted, nose-drippy battle along slippery asphalt. In tune with such contrasts, Mark Cavendish surged to his 100th professional stage win while his compatriot and old friend Bradley Wiggins was dropped by the peloton as it pressed forward relentlessly to catch five breakaways. The Team Sky leader finished a forlorn 3 minutes and 17 seconds back, dropping to 13th place – a full 5 minutes and 22 seconds adrift of the man hogging the *maglia rosa*, Vincenzo Nibali.

'It's a long time since I've seen Brad dropped on the flat,' said Brailsford, after announcing that Rigoberto Urán, lying third overall, would take over the team leadership. 'When he opened the curtains this morning, feeling sick, the last thing he wanted to see was the pouring rain. He showed a lot of courage to try to battle through the stage.'

Confirmation came that Wiggins was struggling physically. Earlier in the race he had told the media that he had caught a cold; he updated them when it turned into a chest infection. He was facing up to the fact that it had become very serious. 'Christian Knees, Danny Pate and Bradley Wiggins all had upper respiratory tract infections with a productive cough,' explained Richard Freeman. 'A lot of people had it in the peloton and they'd cough on the floor, cough on the move. It was horrible. Another rider from another team had already been sent home. Bradley did his best. He didn't want to give up, but the peloton is a damp, cold place to be. He was on antibiotics, but we weren't getting on top of his infection.'

Others had watched him silently fight this predicament. 'For the last few days you could see he was really suffering, but everybody was hoping for the best,' said Ljungqvist.

'I had the same chest infection, but I had a little bit of luck in that mine started on the rest day,' confirmed Knees. 'Also, in the mountains, my job is done early in the stage and I could go easier and rest until the finish line. But, in Bradley's position as team leader and GC contender, he needed to push hard every day. He couldn't hide. He was the Tour de France winner and Olympic champion. He couldn't go easy even for a day to allow his body to recover. He did everything he could.'

'It's one bike race of many. Ultimately, someone had to make a decision. Health is more important than bike racing. That was my job, to take myself out of the bubble of the close-knit team and make an objective decision,' said Freeman. 'Bradley wasn't for giving up. It was an immense disappointment when I ordered, recommended, demanded, asked Bradley to go home.'

STAGE 12

STAGE 13

There were no farewells, no hugs nor handshakes. Bradley just didn't get on the bus. Ryder Hesjedal did not sign on at the start, either. Vincenzo Nibali declared that Cadel Evans was now his main rival as the two winners of 2012 Grand Tours, the Briton and the Canadian who had been pitted against each other as intense Giro rivals, beat a desolate retreat to the airport.

'It was a big letdown. I felt that for him,' said Danny Pate, who moved his seat from the back of the team bus to take over Wiggins's front berth. 'I'd seen all the work he'd done. That guy, I've never seen so much focus. He kind of redefined the word "focus" for me. He had trained so much. His diet was so regimented. It was mind boggling. So it seemed cruel that some stupid little sickness took him away. He'd fought it so hard. He'd had the one bad day on the road and that night, oh, he looked so sick at dinner he could hardly speak . . . I assumed he wouldn't be starting the next day. It was no surprise to me.'

The swap to Rigoberto Urán as leader was not unprecedented. The Colombian had assumed leadership status on Stage 8 of the 2011 Tour de France when Wiggins fell and broke his collarbone. 'I took over as leader and was having a good Tour, wearing the white young rider's jersey from Stage 14. Five days later I lost it after picking up an illness,' recalled Urán. 'Two years later I was also in a good position here, riding as leader now . . . and I was hoping I wasn't going to have the same disappointment.'

'In 2010, Bradley's exit happened quickly,' said Dave Brailsford. 'One minute everything was going to plan; the next minute he was underneath a pile of bikes and riders, game over. This time it crept up. First his chest infection and knee problem were issues to manage, then they started raising questions; then they worsened. It was a gradual realisation that his physical condition had developed into a race-ending situation. As always in sport, you try to be compassionate, but the race doesn't stop. Swiftly you have to move to Plan B. From the start at Team Sky we tried to develop a mind-set based on the premise that goalposts will move and life's not fair, so let's get on with it. We've trained ourselves not to dwell on things. It can seem ruthless from the outside, but we recognise what needs to be done.'

Dan Hunt vouched for a seamless transition. 'It was business as usual, with a different leader. Rigo was right up there on the GC and took all his energy into his new role. He's a great guy, fun, full of energy, always talking, full of beans, always with a million and one things going on. He moves around the peloton really well and is tough and gutsy. He really dogs it out – he's a fantastic bike rider and a super guy to have around. The guys loved racing for him.'

'It was a big disappointment that Brad left, but we still had Rigo,' continued Pate. 'He's relaxed, he comes race-ready. He's completely the opposite personality. He's super-funny, a little chatterbox, where Brad can be subdued and quiet. I think the feeling of the whole team was that it wasn't a bummer because Rigo was in contention and Brad's sickness was something out of our control. It was bad luck. The leader switch didn't bother me. Personally, when I like someone, it's far easier doing dangerous things on a bike and taking risks on their behalf. It goes beyond pay cheques – and Rigo is super-likeable.'

And so the Team Sky operation moved on, maintaining position on another sprint day won by Cavendish, and attracting a new following. 'We picked up a whole new fan club. There'd be 40 or 50 Colombian fans and journalists outside the bus,' said Hunt. 'And a lot of new banter after the *Gazzetta dello Sport* christened Urán "Mick Jagger", which he pretended he didn't get.'

'Oh, he got it!' laughed Pate. 'I just don't know if he liked it that much!'

STAGE 14

Che sorpresa! The weather played havoc on the first of the two scheduled back-to-back summit finishes, forcing the organisers to cancel the climb to the ski resort of Sestriere, re-routing it further along the Val di Susa. Dense low cloud affected visibility, grounding the helicopters that provide a buzz of excitement over the peloton as they relay aerial shots for television. Rigged up in wet-weather gear, the riders endured a damp, soggy day, at one with the elements. 'It was depressing rather than difficult,' said Pate. 'Non-stop rain makes it miserable and dangerous rather than the horrible experience it is in freezing temperatures.'

Road captain Knees prides himself on not being affected by the weather, but he was pleased about the last-minute route change. 'I have to say they made a good call in re-routing so that we finished up the climb. I was wearing my rain jacket but didn't need gloves until the last climb when I was taking it easy, my job done. I worked hard that day and took up a lot of the running at the front with Xabi. The breakaway was a long way ahead, and not many other teams were riding full gas. At times it felt like we were the only team pulling.'

The final climb to Jafferau was where everything shook down. A seven-man breakaway had a ten-minute lead at one point, before the peloton, led by Astana and Team Sky, started reeling them in. With 5km to go, Sergio

Henao attacked but was thwarted. Freezing fog descended and the Italians Mauro Santambrogio and Nibali traded attacks, with the former outsmarting the race leader to take stage glories. Urán, riding without gloves, came in fifth, 30 seconds down, and remained in third place overall.

In *Maglia Rosa: Triumph and Tragedy at the Giro d'Italia*, cycling historian Herbie Sykes concludes: 'You never know where [the Giro] will take you but you can be assured that the journey will be eventful and magical and exasperating and surprising and human.' For Team Sky collectively, it had so far been a predominantly eventful and exasperating passage. With Urán, buoyant after a first Grand Tour stage win and treasuring his particular affinity for the Italian mountains and people, it could turn into something magical, surprising and human. With great courage, the Colombian left his home country as a teenager to make his living as a professional rider in Italy. The experience left him with a deep love for the country and the cultural significance of the Giro. 'I love everything about the Giro. It feels so emotional to be involved in it,' he said. 'The climbs are special. The race is special. The fans are special. The Dolomites are beautiful and the style of climbing suits me.'

Urán came to Europe in 2006 when he was 19 to ride for a small Italian outfit, Team Tenax. 'I turned

professional here, training in the mountains in the north and living in a small apartment I rented in the house of a family in Brescia,' he continued. 'We had a close rapport. They treated me like their adopted son. When I had a bad accident at the Deutschland Tour – I smashed into a wall and fractured my collarbone, elbows, right arm and wrist – the family came and stayed with me in hospital, bathing me, feeding me, nursing me back to health. I live in Pamplona [in Spain] now, but I maintain close ties with Italy. I come and stay with my family and friends, and my fan club is based there.'

To take on the leadership role at the Giro was not something to be taken lightly, Urán said, especially at a number one outfit like Team Sky. 'It's never great to see your leader go and receive the baton of responsibility after someone else's bad luck. You have to respond to the extra burden. Some guys can take it. Some guys can't. To be a leader, you can never have a bad day. You have to be ultra-consistent. That's a huge pressure in a sport where your body is pushed to the limit. You can go from 40 degrees on the coast to –10 degrees up in the mountains. It's crazy. Waking up on those first few days as leader, I felt calm and relaxed. I knew I had prepared extremely well, trained well. I had come into the race with good form and I was confident I could race as hard as I could.

'But I suffered at Sestrieres. It rained and rained. There was non-stop water for five hours and the stage was very difficult. I felt tired. My legs were heavy, but I had a responsibility not to stop pedalling. The cold and bad weather has become another "rival" to defeat in this year's Giro!'

This stage featured two of the truly brutal climbs of the 2013 Giro, as the race made its only deviation from Italy, crossing the frontier to borrow a pair of the Tour de France's most notorious landmarks. First up was the long and demoralising 25.5km up the Category-1 Col du Mont Cenis, which has as its reward a stunning Alpine lake to rhapsodise over, but was otherwise an early leg-sapper, ensuring that the second celebrated climb – the infamous 2,645m Col du Galibier – would deal out its trademark shuffle of the general classification. Even the world's best riders admit they struggle the entire way up the pass, which is tackled via the Col du Télégraphe. The 2013 sequencing of stages heralded full-on racing. With a rest day to follow, there was no reason for riders to hold back.

To the accompaniment of mystical music, TV coverage showcased the scene with surreal shots of fog swirling and clearing to reveal seemingly unreachable jagged peaks. Sub-zero temperatures were forecast. Team cars were banned from sounding their horns for fear of triggering avalanches. Few fans braved the cold; some hearty souls came, left a Union flag mounted on a snow bank and retreated to cheer the riders in spirit.

There were mutterings that the riders were unhappy with the conditions set for the descent of the Col du Mont Cenis and fears that the fabled Galibier climb would be cancelled. Earlier, entrenched winter deposits had been cleared with snowploughs and explosives. Confirmation came that the stage would not finish at the summit, but 4.25km further down the climb. This meant the next conqueror of the Galibier would throw his arms up in celebration by the new memorial to Marco Pantani, whose triumph in 1998 ranks as one of the most iconic moments in cycling, achieved on his way to becoming the last man to win the Giro and Tour de France double.

As the peloton pedalled from verdant valley to the monotone granite-and-snow high-alpine landscape, the temperature plummeted. Cold itself acts as a competitive filter. Riders take knocks earlier when energy is used up simply in keeping warm, not pedalling. You have to get the clothing right, the food right, and judge it spot on to be able to go and 'race', rather than just get through it. 'There's always a big difference in how the riders deal with the cold.

STAGE 15

Some suffer, others ride without gloves,' said Ljungqvist, while Danny Pate had his own theory on performance-to-conditions outcome. Coming from Colorado, home to some of the world's best ski resorts, you would have expected him to feel at home. 'It's a different kind of cold because it's so wet. In Colorado, it's a dry climate,' he protested. 'If you watch the races, it's guys from climates similar to the prevailing conditions who win. If it starts raining, all the Dutch and Belgian guys come in first . . .'

Physiologically, this was where Team Sky's weeks spent training at altitude camp in Tenerife paid off. On the day it was a matter of appropriate clothing. 'Clothing is key to managing the cold and wet weather – ensuring access to garments that are fit-for-purpose and optimised for performance in various weather conditions, but also

managing clothing within the race – making sure the right garment is available when required, that the riders can get the garments from the team car when needed with minimal effort, and also shed them when no longer needed,' said Tim Kerrison, head of performance support. 'Having the correct protection from the elements can not only make an immediate impact on performance, but can also affect the health of the riders – and weather-related illnesses had a big impact on the peloton in the Giro.'

This was a stage when outside observers glimpsed borderline madness in a rider's mindset. Cue, Christian Knees: 'I had a nice moment when my legs felt good and I was still in the group at the Col du Télégraphe going up towards the Galibier. I was next to Cadel Evans, so I asked Rigo loudly on the radio if the race was hard enough for

him or whether I should make the tempo harder. Cadel Evans looked at me – his face just said, "You're crazy!"'

'It turned out to be a hard one, as expected,' reported Ljungqvist. 'The riders made a gentlemen's agreement not to race over the first climb and then when the GPM [Gran Premio della Montagna] came, they started attacking. A group went away and then it was a full-on race. We tried to attack with Sergio on the Télégraphe to set up a stage win, but with a complete white-out in the final 4km, there wasn't enough road. Visconti rode away and finished alone.'

Movistar's Giovanni Visconti, who shares his birthday – January 13 – with the late Pantani, was one of a group of six who jumped away near the top of the Col du Mont Cenis on a quest for mountains points and who then increased their advantage on the run to the foot of the Col du Télégraphe. The Italian went clear of the group on the Télégraphe, spectacularly clearing the summit with a lead of 40 seconds. He maintained his advantage all the way to the finish. Afterwards, having waved the Tricolore and received champagne from podium girls dressed in skiwear, he remained incredulous: 'I can't believe I won on such a mythical climb as this.'

There was no loitering for the others. Urán, who came in tenth alongside Nibali and Evans, quickly jumped into a warm car to change into dry clothes. 'My freezer in Colombia isn't as cold as it is up here,' he joked. 'Fortunately I've got used to the cold after racing in Europe for several years, but what *frio*! We've had two tough days, but today was great racing.'

STAGE 16

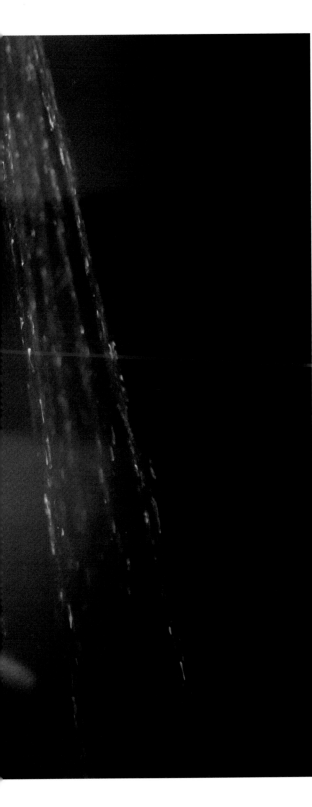

After a rest day that gave the riders a chance to recover – and quietly acknowledge that this was one of the toughest Giros for years – came a stage that was frazzling in its deceptiveness. In theory, it was downhill, followed by a long flat stretch to Ivrea, north-east of Turin, but 'downhill' meant a fearsome descent of the Col du Télégraphe, followed by another hard climb up and down the Col du Mont Cenis, and then a taunting kick-up at Andrate before the cruise to the finish line.

'It was crazy,' said Pate. 'I was trying to get into a breakaway and stay all the way until the finish line. Add in a Category-1 descent and it's hectic – you're going single-file downhill at full speed. When we hit the valley road, the peloton divided into three; Rigo was in a 'relaxed' position in the peloton, so I had to stop and wait for him. To get in and stay in the breakaway had been a big effort, and the split was a little unexpected, but through teamwork we could recover from that position. We got right back to Rigo and Christian – Dario and I helped him re-group. Depending on the stage's profile, or the team's tactics, a breakaway can be a chance for a rider to attack a stage as part of a small group working together in order to open a gap from the peloton. More often than not the escape party is reeled in, but sometimes a solo bid for glory is successful. To win from a breakaway is a peculiarly satisfying triumph and therein lies the mysterious politicking involved in breakaway dynamics, as Pate's recall suggests. 'I was able to get in the breakaway because of the profile of the stage, and our group broke away further into a leader group. We were going well until the last three guys came across, including Damiano Caruso, who was lying 18th overall. That was too bad for our break. Some of the others were angry when they saw him come up. It tainted the whole break because Katusha and RadioShack decided to take it up. It was a huge letdown and ruined all that we'd accomplished.'

Team leader Urán held station, powering in with the leading group 14 seconds behind Beñat Intxausti's successful burst for the line. 'Rigoberto is going well,' commented Ljungqvist. 'We're still taking it day by day, still looking to move up.'

Nearing halfway point of the final week, the riders had so far had sprints, time trials, mountains, rest days, sunshine, rainstorms and blizzards. They had spent three weeks cooped up with one another in a high-pressure environment, where every meal, massage, bus transfer, warm-up, sign-on and race plan was precisely scheduled. It was tough going. Sleep doesn't come easily at altitude in the mountains – even for the exhausted.

A day for the sprinters dawned over a route billed in one preview as 'flat, more flat, a decent lump and then more flat'. The start was 50km from the home of charismatic joker Kanstantsin Siutsou, prompting a party atmosphere with friends, family and tiny son who hitched a lift on Dad's bike. This was the community that chanted 'Sky, Sky' as Kosta made his recuperatory forays on local roads last autumn after breaking his leg in the Tour de France. The buzz generated by this pocket of support was a timely boost for the riders who were now 19 days into the grind of a Grand Tour.

'It's hard. You're away from home for a month. As each stage ends you begin the process of getting ready for the next stage, when all you want to do is go to sleep,' said Pate. 'You might have two or three hours' driving to get to the next hotel, then a massage – which sounds relaxing, but can be painful – and dinner, which is the highlight. We're staying in small, old hotels, but the carers drive ahead so that we have our own mattresses and bedding. That consistency is nice. You're cocooned in the Team Sky world and it's a luxury. The team expect a certain level of performance from us and in turn provide us with a certain level of care and support.'

While carers rub and knead muscles, apply kinesiology tape and prepare bidons, and mechanics wash and service the bikes, Søren Kristiansen, the team chef, prepares psychologically comforting food in cahoots with nutritionist Nigel Mitchell. 'The riders need to perform on a daily basis, based on recovery. Nutrition is the key in that recovery process,' explained Mitchell. 'The number of calories required depends on the rider and the day's demands – somewhere between 4,500 and 9,000. It can be hard work eating and riding, eating and riding. To make it easier we use juices, which is a neat way of getting nutrients as well as rehydration. Søren takes 30kg of vegetables each day to create litres of juice.'

The team doctor is on call 24 hours a day. Before breakfast each rider goes to his room to be weighed. If there's a risk of dehydration, a urine sample is taken. After breakfast each rider is assessed, with the physio on hand. Dressings are changed and made more comfortable for racing. During the race the doctor sits in the race car, ready to treat anyone with a headache, troublesome saddle sores or a lost inhaler. 'If someone's fallen off, I'm there on site to assess them,' said Freeman. 'If it's serious, I'll accompany them to hospital. If it's not, I'll monitor them once they're back in the saddle and make sure the decision to race on was the right one.'

At the finish, Freeman accompanies the riders to doping control. On the bus, grazes are rubbed with iodine and dressed, and food and rehydration drinks are provided. 'Back at the hotel, I check their weights and compare them to their morning figure. Half the team go to the *soigneurs* for massage while the other half eat. They then swap over. I check them individually and do a final round of their rooms at 10pm. Someone might have a headache or a loose stomach, or have difficulty sleeping. In the middle of night I might get a call from someone experiencing leg spasms or abdominal pain. And the day starts again . . .'

STAGE 17

By now, observers were saying Vincenzo Nibali was running out of opportunities to lose this race. 'We kept hoping he'd have a bad day,' said Christian Knees. 'But he was racing so well.' The arrival of the tortuous uphill individual time trial, however, coincided with forecasts of apocalyptic weather for Stages 19 and 20: heavy snow was expected to fall above 1,500m and temperatures were due to be well below freezing. Could Cadel Evans or Rigoberto Urán get close to the *maglia rosa* and set up a thriller in the last few days? Could this be the point at which Nibali slipped up or blew a gasket?

Thanks to the devices that display and record the SRM power-output data, no Team Sky rider was in danger of burning out. Each rider knew the numbers required to perform in sprint mode, and could refer to the data that gives constant feedback of their speed, cadence, heart rate and power to help guide their pace and intensity. 'On key sections we also feed back some aspects of the riders' performance to help them to better understand how they are coping with and responding to the demands of the stage,' explained Tim Kerrison.

Urán, still in third place in the overall standings, lay 2 minutes and 46 seconds behind Nibali and a potentially bridgeable 1 minute and 20 seconds behind Evans in second place. With four days left to battle for gains – and to survive any inopportune incident – Team Sky's immediate goal was to focus on leapfrogging the Australian to claim second spot. At only 20.6km, the stage was not long enough for decisive gaps to be opened up. Although predominantly uphill, its demands suited a time-trial specialist rather than an out-and-out climber. 'We hope Rigo can produce a very strong ride. He's feeling good, he's relatively fresh and he's looking to perform. It will be nice to see what he can do,' said Ljungqvist.

The bad news for those pursuing Nibali was that the Italian had been criticised in the Italian press for not winning a stage and had attended the sign-on radiating vibes of extra motivation. Evans is always a reliable time trialler, so how would Urán fare? As if setting up the drama between the podium-place claimants, dark clouds rolled in and shed rain just as Urán, then Evans and finally Nibali set off at intervals on a lap of the local velodrome in Mori

STAGE 18

before heading uphill to push themselves through the pain barrier as they wrestled with the clock.

Walk past the room Urán and Henao share in hotels at night and you will hear party music, but the Colombian is a serious professional. He had studied the course on video, recce'd it and noted where the toughest sections came nearer the end. It would be a matter of going full gas once he hit the climb, giving it his all. At the first time-check things didn't look promising for the Team Sky man, but as the gradient steepened his climber's legs came into their own. He finished a valiant sixth, leaving him a mere 10 seconds behind Cadel Evans in the general classification – perfectly poised to pounce in the high mountains.

Nibali positively flew to Polsa, winning the stage with a supreme show of power and concentration to silence the press. He beat the next fastest man over the course, Samuel Sánchez, by 58 seconds and stretched his lead over Evans to more than 4 minutes.

'It was a really good performance from Rigo. He paced himself well there and got a strong result,' said Ljungqvist, as a smiling Urán spoke to the phalanx of Colombian media and went to warm down. 'We'll see what happens now with the two mountain stages but it really gives us something to fight for. We know they will be two hard days – regardless of how the stages are run – with the weather. We're getting towards the end of the race and we want to leave it all out there and really go for it.'

The sight of Cadel Evans reaching the finish line in 25th place was heartening for Team Sky. He had come to the Giro with only a five-week window of preparation, calling his entry an 'experiment', but he had clung terrier-like to second place. Were his legs now giving up on him? Would that work in Urán's favour going into the Dolomites? You couldn't read much into the BMC man's Twitter utterance: 'Uphill TT done here at the Giro: Nibali in a class of his own. Evans – if I may say so myself – abysmal.' Maybe it had just galvanised the Australian?

The riders went to bed visualising a significant re-route to the first of the back-to-back summit finishes in the Dolomites. Out had gone the Passo di Gavia and the mythical Passo dello Stelvio because of snow at the summits; in came three climbs – the Category-2 Passo del Tonale, which rises at a steady gradient before a significant drop to the foot of the first of two Category-1 ascents, the short and vertiginous Passo Castrin and the final 22km climb up the Val Martello. The riders woke up, jumped on the doctor's scales and headed down to breakfast where they learnt that a fresh dump of snow meant the stage had been cancelled. It was the first Giro stage to be called off in a quarter of a century.

'That was a great day!' said Danny Pate. 'And it was much better to be told first thing than being told at the start, at the very last minute. We got the message at breakfast. Normally, you get up, have breakfast, get on the bus, go through the team presentation of the profile with the *directeurs sportifs*, and have three hours staring at a daunting profile thinking, "Oh, man, this is going to be a terrible day." But we didn't have that. I was awake for probably half an hour when I got the message. It was like a third rest day . . . That day was great!'

With the race set to resume the following day with a mountain-stage decider that incorporated five categorised climbs from Silandro to the Tre Cime di Lavaredo, the teams jumped on their indoor trainers. It's important to open up the blood flow in the legs for a few hours on rest days otherwise they feel 'blocked' the following day. The day's respite also gave the doctor and physio time to investigate and treat any ongoing issues.

Vincenzo Nibali's Astana used their hotel's underground garage as a makeshift gym; other teams commandeered lobbies and corridors. Conversation was not in short supply following the announcement that Danilo Di Luca had tested positive for EPO, news that prompted universal dismay and condemnation. 'It beggared belief for him to test positive after returning from a previous ban,' said Brailsford. 'In my opinion the penalties in our sport are currently too lenient. A penalty for a first offence should pose a much greater deterrent. And anyone who commits a second offence has no place in this sport.'

Meanwhile, rider safety in the high mountains remained an issue. 'The weather on this race has been the worst that I've seen at a Grand Tour,' said Marcus Ljungqvist. 'Everybody knew the risk of high-mountain finishes in May in the Dolomites, but I don't think anybody expected it to be this bad. It would have been great with good weather on clear roads with the scenery and the helicopter shots, but it's about making a good race that's

STAGE 19

safe for the riders. Tomorrow, we could be in a similar
situation again. The route has even higher passes. It will be
a last-minute decision again to see what happens.'

STAGE 20

People come from all over the world to see the play of light on the dramatic, battlement-like cliffs of the Tre Cime di Lavaredo ('the three peaks of Lavaredo'). The near-vertical Cima Grande – the highest of the peaks – was not ascended until 1869, and its northern wall counts as one of the six great north faces of the Alps. Even after the re-routing of this penultimate stage – with the removal of the Passo di Costalunga, Passo San Pellegrino and Passo di Giau climbs – the challenge of triumphing up the monstrous gradient, at altitude, in the snow, was according to Nibali 'going to be a dream come true for someone'.

For Team Sky, Stage 20 represented the best chance to see Urán jump up to second place. 'We saw that Nibali was the best. He'd shown that,' said Pate. 'Plan A was Rigo wins the stage; Plan B was to ensure Rigo got second place overall. A win–win.'

'It was absolutely freezing, but I knew what I wanted to do,' said Urán. 'I wanted to make the team proud, I wanted to work with maximum effort for myself, I wanted to do it for Colombia. My country is having a boom period in cycling and I am proud to be Colombian. With Cadel only 10 seconds in front, my goal was to try to win the stage – and then it would be a double victory to move up to second overall. I was so focused I didn't feel the cold. But with the conditions being so difficult – and Nibali proving so strong – the stage win was always going to be a hard goal to achieve.

'When I saw Cadel get into difficulties I dug deep, concentrated my efforts on capturing second place and gave it everything. I felt no joy at the top, just satisfaction. This Giro has been a long, long journey. We were all absolutely knackered, fighting for position, but there's also huge relief. We've done it! It's me who takes this second place. But it's thanks to the great work of the team that allowed me to do so, not just today – helping to protect and position me – but also during the whole three weeks, and I am very grateful for their support.'

So the dream came true for Nibali, who attacked on the final climb, with only Urán and two other Colombians – Fabio Duarte and Carlos Betancur – able to muster some fight. The Italian crossed the line in driving snow to clinch the stage win and all but seal a convincing overall victory, with just the sprint-friendly stage into Brescia to come. 'In the snow, the cold, it felt like an infinite finish,' he said poetically.

With Zandio and Henao also defying the painful sting of snow on bare skin to finish in the top 30, Team Sky had also effectively clinched the team classification. For all the riders, it was the toughest of finishes. 'They were in a state at the end. It was super-, super-cold, but we did all the emergency measures to prevent hypothermia,' said Ljungqvist. 'They didn't shower. They had to keep their clothes on, get on the warm bus. If they're alive on the bus, we know they're OK! Rigo really suffers in the cold, yet today he did great.'

Blue skies, sunshine, bottles of prosecco offered from the team-car window. No, it wasn't a mirage induced by three head-spinning weeks of tireless racing; it was the final and largely processional journey into Brescia. With three of the four classifications decided heading into the leisurely last day, all attention was on the fight for red as the 96th edition of the Giro concluded in clouds of pink confetti and balloons. Team Sky, all business settled with Rigoberto Urán's magnificent second place and the team-classification win, could sit back and enjoy the sight of former team member Mark Cavendish winning the sprint title and joining the cycling greats who have won the points classification in all three Grand Tours.

After three weeks, there was quite a tally of team achievements to celebrate. 'Credit to all of them, and to all the peloton. It was not fun, riding in these conditions, but everyone coped with it very well,' said Marcus Ljungqvist. 'Everyone came in with a goal. Rigoberto really stepped up. He was very relaxed . . . sometimes, too relaxed! When he works for someone else in the mountains, he's absolutely selfless, but when he gets the opportunity to go for it

STAGE 21

himself, he really delivers. It was a huge achievement for him and it shows how strong the team is. We came in with one leader, and ended up with another who finished second in the GC.'

Urán's second place in the general classification was the highest Team Sky finish in the Giro d'Italia to date, and the Colombian's runner-up status was all the more admirable for being just behind an invincible winner in Vincenzo Nibali. As Dan Hunt commented, 'Nibali had upped his game over the winter. His performances were super in all races all year. He'd been a level above all season. He beat Froomey (in Tirreno–Adriatico in Italy) and Brad in the Giro del Trentino.' Ljungqvist agreed: 'He was super-motivated after last year's Tour. He was riding for a new team, at his home Grand Tour; he was on another level, untouchable. It was just a pity we didn't get to see a race between a 100 per cent fit Bradley and Nibali.'

The team classification was a just reward for the indefatigable, good-spirited work of each rider – Dario Cataldo, Sergio Henao, Christian Knees, Danny Pate, Salvatore Puccio, Kanstantsin Siutsou, Rigoberto Urán, Bradley Wiggins and Xabier Zandio. The odds kept stacking up against them, but, day by day, they showed supreme teamwork by getting the maximum out of every situation. The Grand Tour also yielded two superb stage victories: the first in the team time trial on Ischia, which

catapulted Puccio into the *maglia rosa* for a proud day, and the second on Stage 10, when Urán signalled his form with his stirring solo victory on Altopiano del Montasio in the first day of the high mountains.

'The final day in Brescia was super,' said Dan Hunt. 'Second for Rigo was fantastic and the lads deserved the team win. Those were eight very, very tired bodies on the podium. We'd all dealt with a lot of adversity, but they never gave up, never looked back when Brad left. They did as good a job for Rigo as they would have done for Brad.'

'Some may consider it a consolation prize for not winning the overall, but it's a big thing. It shows how strong the team is. It was nice to be up on the podium and get the recognition,' said Danny Pate, speaking on behalf of the *domestiques*. 'I have to say, though, it was a bit of a letdown that there was no champagne. We'd been imagining eight of us up there with a big bottle of champagne – but no!'

'There wasn't much of a celebration, to be honest,' confirmed Ljungqvist. 'The night before, we had a couple of glasses of wine together. The team prize is really nice for the guys and they really deserved that. It was a goal we began to look at later on in the race when it came within reach. So it was great to be able to take it. This Giro was such a team effort, but at the end of the day, it's just another bike race. Everyone wants to get back to their family.'

Just another bike race! On 4 May, the all-consuming battle started for the aptly named *Trofeo Senza Fine* (Endless Trophy) and by 26 May the Giro, the crazy race, the race that rewards fighters, the race that conjures up endless hurdles and setbacks, had dealt its cards. For Team Sky it was a race that team members – from riders to support staff – would remember as 'difficult, but interesting' (Richard Freeman), 'full of highs and lows' (Marcus Ljungqvist), 'surprising' (Rigoberto Urán) and 'a whole new perspective on bad weather and what's acceptable' (Danny Pate).

'The real high was that the strength of the team really shone through,' said Ljungqvist. 'We can't be anything but really happy with second place, the team prize and two stage victories. The pink jersey will have to wait for another time, but at the end of the day the strongest rider won the race. Congratulations to Vincenzo from the whole team. It was a well-deserved win but, for us, second place is a huge achievement, having lost Brad early on.'

As Pate said after Urán's fillip of a win on Stage 10, 'You finish a tough day with a result like that and it makes you look forward to the next one.' The sentiment can be repeated for the race itself: you complete a tough Grand Tour with a sense of achievement and it makes you long for the next one. Team Sky will be back next year for another attempt at the *maglia rosa*. The Giro d'Italia, with all its gruelling challenges and teasing impenetrability, retains its allure.

THE GIRO IN DETAIL

'The moment you think, "This is going to be a regulation stage," then that is the moment of danger. Things can happen at any moment in the Giro. You have to be ready for any kind of attack at any moment.'

Sir Dave Brailsford

ROUTE / A rare road stage on the Naples seafront to decide who first dons the *maglia rosa*. The riders headed away from the Piazza Plebiscito to race four passages of the 16.3km Circuito Lungo before the sprint finale: eight pan-flat laps of the 8km Circuito Corto. A nailed-on bunch sprint guaranteed a thrilling fight for pink.

HOW IT UNFOLDED / As soon as the flag dropped under sunny skies Omega Pharma-Quick Step controlled the peloton, with seven riders heading up the road. After the escapees had battled it out for the mountain points over two passes of the day's single Category-4 climb on the Via Francesco Petrarca, teams prepared to vie for position at the front of the bunch in the final 25km.

Xabier Zandio, Danny Pate and Christian Knees drove Team Sky along on the final eight laps. Nine riders were

in a position to contest the sprint finish, with OP-QS's Mark Cavendish forced to freestyle to claim victory and become the first recipient of the leader's jersey.

A tricky, crash-filled opener, but Team Sky made it to the finish without issues. A split of 18 seconds formed between the sprinters and the peloton, with Sir Bradley Wiggins safely home in the latter, awarded the same time as his GC rivals after the 3km rule was applied.

STAGE 1 RESULT:

Winner. Mark Cavendish (GB);
Omega Pharma-Quick Step; 02h 58' 38"
2. Elia Viviani (Ita); Cannondale; @ same time
3. Nacer Bouhanni (Fra); FDJ; @ same time

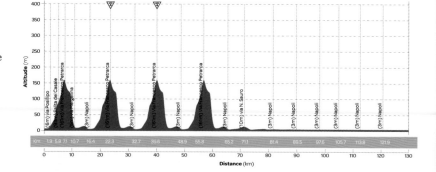

Stage 1
THE QUEST BEGINS
Saturday 4 May / Naples to Naples, 130km

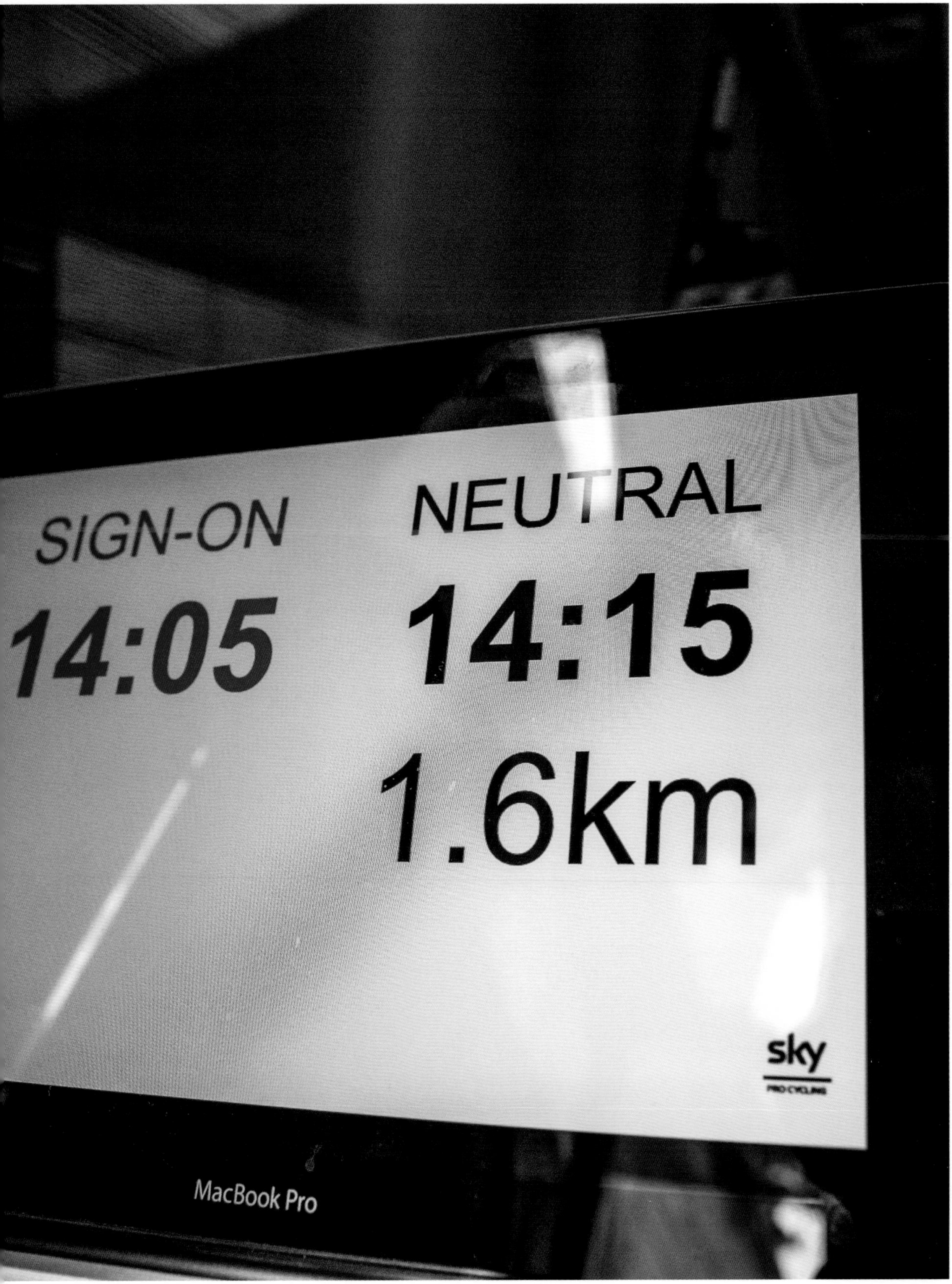
SIGN-ON
14:05
NEUTRAL
14:15
1.6km
sky
MacBook Pro

ROUTE / The beautiful island of Ischia hosted a showpiece team time trial. Time gaps were not expected to be significant on the short route, which hugged the north coast before looping inland to cut off the north-west corner of the island. It was a largely flat stage, but included climbs either side of the intermediate time check in Casamicciola Terme that could easily blow a team apart.

HOW IT UNFOLDED / Team Sky produced an incredible performance, measuring the tough course perfectly, finishing with five riders in a winning time of 22 minutes and 5 seconds – enough to see Salvatore Puccio in the symbolic *maglia rosa*, a magical moment for the 23-year-old Italian, who also took the white young rider's jersey.

Blanco Pro Cycling set the early pace with a time of 22 minutes and 33 seconds.

Team Sky's time proved to be 9 seconds quicker than anyone else, with Movistar clocking the second fastest time and Astana rounding out the podium. The result placed five Team Sky riders in the top five overall, with Puccio heading Wiggins, Henao, Cataldo and Urán – all five riders crossing the line together at the finish. Earlier in the stage Pate, Knees, Siutsou and Zandio each, in turn, gave it their all to set up the team for a fast finish.

STAGE 2 RESULT:

Winner. Team Sky (22:05)

2. Movistar + 0.00.09"

3. Astan + 0.00.14"

OVERALL STANDINGS:

1. Salvatore Puccio (Ita); Team Sky; 03h 20'43"

2. Bradley Wiggins (GB); Team Sky; @ same time

3. Sergio Henao (Col); Team Sky; @ same time

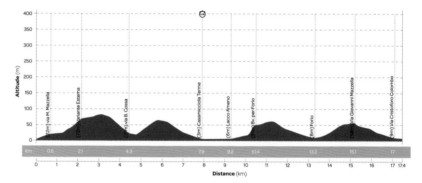

Stage 2
FORMATION FLYING
Sunday 5 May / Ischia to Forio, 17.4km, Team Time Trial

ROUTE / The first foray into medium mountains. After hugging the coast on the run down to the foot of Italy, the final 40km stretch tested the peloton with two categorised climbs. A tense chase back on the descent would set up an exciting finish.

HOW IT UNFOLDED / A seven-man group broke clear and built up a lead of almost seven minutes, but the gap began to tumble after 153km as a peloton led by Team Sky powered its way on the climb up San Mauro Cilento.

The race blew to pieces on the final hurdle of Sella di Cantona, catching out a number of top riders in a breathless grandstand finish. Luca Paolini won by 16 seconds to establish a 17-second overall lead after a much tougher finale than forecast. Defending champion Ryder Hesjedal had launched the first

of a number of attacks, and finished just behind Cadel Evans in the sprint for the final podium places.

Wiggins made it home safely, measuring his efforts on the technical descent into Marina di Ascea to finish eighth in an elite group of chasers. Urán finished alongside him, moving up to third overall. Henao lost time late on with a minor crash; Puccio spent a memorable day in the *maglia rosa* before slipping back on the final climb.

STAGE 3 RESULT:

Winner. Luca Paolini (Ita); Katyusha; 05h 43' 50"

2. Cadel Evans (Aus); BMC Racing; @ 00' 16"

3. Ryder Hesjedal (Can); Garmin; @ 00' 16"

OVERALL STANDINGS:

1. Luca Paolini (Ita); Katusha; 09h 04' 32"

2 Bradley Wiggins (GB); Sky; @ 00' 17"

3 Rigoberto Uran (Col); Sky; @ 00' 17"

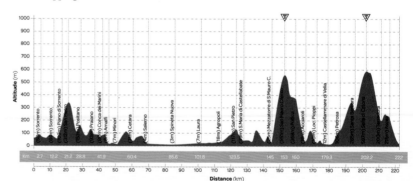

Stage 3
PAOLINI IN PINK
Monday 6 May / Sorrento to Marina di Ascea, 212km

ROUTE / The second-longest stage took the riders down the Mediterranean coast to the most southerly point of the Giro. A kick in the tail came in the last 35k in the looming form of Vibo Valentia, a Category-3 climb, followed by the Category-2 Croce Ferrata. Not a summit finish, though; the stage leader had just under 7km to defend on the downhill run into Serra San Bruno.

HOW IT UNFOLDED / Seven riders headed up the road early as Katusha committed numbers to support Paolini and the pink jersey. Heading into the final 100km, the breakaway split in two and the gap – close to 8 minutes – quickly came down. Rain and fog shrouded the climb of Vibo Valentia as the catch was made. Team Sky set the pace on the final climb with Siutsou, Henao and Urán supporting Wiggins.

Paolini remained well positioned on to the final ascent, but the stage came down to a shoot-out after a drama-filled descent that saw the peloton fracture, Nibali require a wheel change and Wiggins get caught behind a crash. Enrico Battaglin won the sprint to the line.

The result saw Urán move up to second overall, Wiggins drop to sixth and Henao round out the team's presence in the top ten by sitting in eighth overall, 37 seconds back.

STAGE 4 RESULT:

Winner. Enrico Battaglin (Ita); Bardiani Valvole; 06h 14' 19"

2. Fabio Felline (Ita); Androni Giocattoli; @ same time

3. Giovanni Visconti (Ita); Movistar; @ same time

OVERALL STANDINGS:

1. Luca Paolini (Ita); Katusha; 15h 18' 51"

2. Rigoberto Urán (Col); Team Sky; +00' 17"

3. Benat Intxausti (Esp); Movistar; +00' 26"

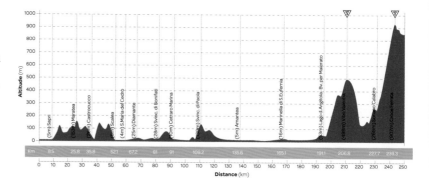

Stage 4
A BIG DAY OUT
Tuesday 7 May / Policastro Bussentino to Serra San Bruno, 246km

ROUTE / After the Cant. San Salvatore climb at 44.8km, the route north up the coast was pan-flat – or *piatta come una tavola*, as they say in these parts – until the brief Montescaglioso ascent and the final kick-up into Matera spiced things up.

HOW IT UNFOLDED / An inconspicuous start, then a wrestle for supremacy on the slope up the first big climb as every team wanted to be towards the front going over the top. Team Sky powered up on behalf of Wiggins, Urán and Henao according to plan, but Urán suffered a puncture on the descent. Pate gave him his wheel, while Puccio, Zandio and Cataldo helped the Colombian rejoin the peloton, getting him there 100m before the last climb.

Henao sprinted to fourth place after a dramatic conclusion in Matera. Urán, Team Sky's other Colombian, was positioned towards the front of a reduced

peloton heading into the final kilometre when a crash on a tight left-hand corner decimated the field, sending riders careering into the barriers. Henao was among the few unaffected and crossed the line in a 12-man group after John Degenkolb secured victory.

With the crash taking place inside the last three kilometres, all the main GC contenders were credited with the same time as the winner, which ensured the overall standings remained unchanged.

STAGE 5 RESULT:

Winner. John Degenkolb (Ger); Argos-Shimano; 04h 37' 48"

2. Ángel Vicioso (Esp); Katusha; @ same time

3. Paul Martens (Ger); Blanco Pro Cycling; @ same time

OVERALL STANDINGS:

1. Luca Paolini (Ita); Katusha; 19h 56' 39"

2. Rigoberto Urán (Col); Team Sky; +00' 17"

3. Benat Intxausti (Esp); Movistar; +00' 26"

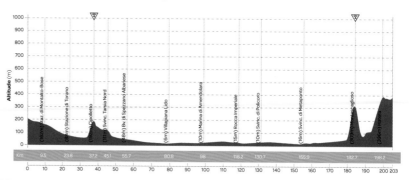

Stage 5
CRASH AT THE CORNER
Wednesday 8 May / Cosenza to Matera, 203km

ROUTE / The last outing for the sprinters for a while, so a hectic day was predicted. The route hugged the coast, encompassing a pair of sprints in Trani and Barletta before the race arrived at the finishing circuit, hosted by Margherita di Savoia. Two laps of the 16.6km Circuito Delle Saline saw the fast men in full-adrenalin mode.

HOW IT UNFOLDED / Australians Cameron Wurf and Jack Bobridge broke away early, establishing a gap of over 6 minutes, but their efforts proved futile on a sprint-friendly route. At 36km from home, OP-QS, FDJ and Orica-GreenEDGE charged to the front to take up launch position for their sprinters. As the peloton reached the first finishing circuit, space became tight and crashes inevitable.

Team Sky had a scare when Wiggins was caught out by the biggest crash. The Briton was being paced back into the bunch after a mechanical problem forced a bike change in the last 30km when a crash ahead blocked the road and lost him valuable time on many GC rivals. Knees ensured the pace was sportingly curtailed up the road and Team Sky rode hard to bring everything back together.

Mark Cavendish produced his trademark late kick to seal his 39th Grand Tour win. The peloton crossed the line with no change in the overall standings.

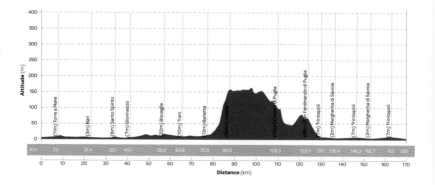

Stage 6
SCARE IN SAVOIA
Thursday 9 May / Mola di Bari to Margherita di Savoia, 169km

ROUTE / From the pancake flatness of Stage 6 to a brutal shark's-jaw profile. The peloton raced north, close to the Adriatic coast through the hills of the Abruzzo region. After 40km, it was goodbye flat terrain. A relentless series of small but steep ramps – including four categorised climbs – presented potential launch pads for decisive attacks. Vigilance required.

HOW IT UNFOLDED / After an initial tussle, six riders went clear and established an advantage of close to 7 minutes. The fugitives came under threat as the pace increased towards the first big climb at Villamagna. The peloton started to split apart under the demands of the wildly undulating route. The rain closed in. Road conditions became treacherous, causing slips and mayhem.

Wiggins was among a significant number of riders to go down, crashing on a perilous hairpin on the descent into Pescara in the final 20km. Nibali, the downhill specialist, had pushed the pace on the plummeting gradient. The Italian crashed himself, but bounced back to finish safely in a lead group of contenders that arrived 1 minute 7 seconds down on stage winner Adam Hansen.

Team Sky battled to limit their losses. Urán and Henao dropped back to pace Wiggins to the line and he crossed it 1 minute 24 seconds further back from his main GC rivals, slipping to 23rd overall.

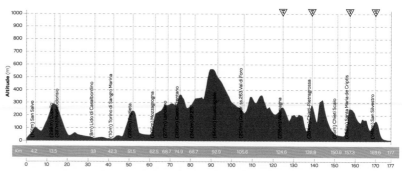

Stage 7
HAZARDOUS HAIRPIN
Friday 10 May/ Marina di San Salvo to Pescara, 177km

ROUTE / A pivotal stage for Wiggins to set the agenda heading into the final two weeks. Down the ramp on to a twisty opening sequence, this test was deceptively technical with plenty of rhythm-busting undulations, notably the ramp up to Novilara and the final climb to the line.

HOW IT UNFOLDED / Former Team Sky rider Alex Dowsett set the time to beat – 1hr 16' 27" – and spent a tense few hours watching others push themselves up the final drag to try to match it.

Wiggins blasted down the ramp aboard his new Pinarello Bolide, but a puncture forced him to change machine during the damp and winding first section. Only 13th quickest through the first intermediate, he got into his rhythm and finished a strong second, 10 seconds down on his fellow Briton in a performance that brought him back up to fourth overall.

While stage victory was the aim, Wiggins put time into all of his GC rivals. New race leader Nibali would take an advantage of 1 minute 16 seconds into the mountains. Cadel Evans moved up to second overall. Hesjedal dropped 2 minutes 23 seconds to sit sixth overall. Team Sky's Colombian duo, Henao and Urán, continued their strong campaigns, finishing ninth and twelfth to elevate themselves to seventh and tenth overall. Cataldo's 30th-place finish represented an impressive return from illness.

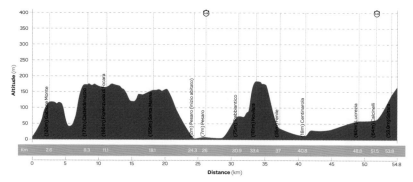

Stage 8
MIXED EMOTIONS
Saturday 11 May / Gabicce Mare to Saltara, 54.8km, Individual Time Trial

ROUTE / A tough medium-mountain stage before the rest day. The opening 65km offered a warm-up prior to the Category-2 Passo della Consuma, followed by the Category-1 Vallombrosa, and two further tests of legs 22km and 11km from the finish line.

HOW IT UNFOLDED / Maxim Belkov took victory in a demanding stage that had always looked likely to play into the hands of a breakaway. The Russian weathered attacks from fellow escapees on the climbs before unleashing his power over the Vallombrosa and the final third to win by 44 seconds from Carlos Betancur – the Colombian in second place mistakenly celebrating as if he'd won the stage.

Team Sky dug deep in the rain to maintain fourth place for Wiggins, who was paced back to the lead group after slipping back on the technical and treacherously wet descent down Vallombrosa. A tense chase saw the team's GC rivals push the pace fast at the front of the peloton, the gap stretching out to a minute at one point.

Henao and Urán sat in the lead group on the descent and moved up a position to sixth and ninth respectively in the GC fight. Wiggins was able to regroup and limit his losses, finishing safely in a reduced front group to retain fourth place overall, 1 minute 16 seconds behind race leader Nibali.

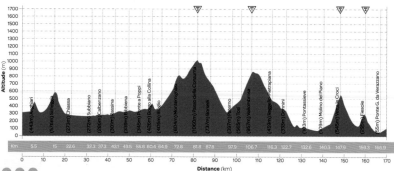

Stage 9
DIGGING DEEP FOR WIGGO
Sunday 12 May / Sansepolcro to Florence, 170km

ROUTE / The race moved to the high mountains of north-east Italy and introduced the first summit finish to shuffle the GC contenders. Untroubling for 90km, the route rose to scale the Passo Cason di Lanza via a stinging maximum gradient of 16 per cent. A handy descent gave legs a rest before the drag up to the finish.

HOW IT UNFOLDED / Rigoberto Urán produced a stunning climbing performance to capture a solo victory – his first Grand Tour stage win – jumping clear on the final ascent of the Altopiano del Montasio.

While 13 riders broke clear of the peloton after 30km, Team Sky pedalled fiercely from the off to pressurise Nibali's Astana. Pate, Zandio, Siutsou and Cataldo pushed the pace throughout an epic test right on to the final climb and isolated the race leader down to one team-mate. Urán picked his moment with 7.5km to go, and scorched through to snatch the stage from compatriot Carlos Betancur.

Unfortunately, Wiggins had slipped back on the steepest section of the first Category-1 ascent and battled thereafter to limit his losses. He finished tenth to drop 1 second behind Urán in the GC, and 2 minutes 5 seconds down on Nibali. The Italian overcame chain problems to finish third on the stage, pushing out his advantage over nearest challenger Cadel Evans.

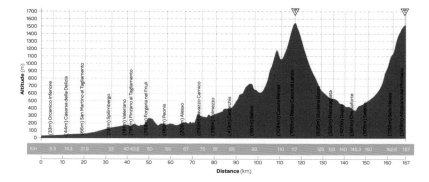

Stage 10
MAJESTIC URÁN
Tuesday 14 May / Cordenons to Altopiano del Montasio, 167km

ROUTE / A medium-mountain stage that for the first 70km was mostly downhill before a long drag up the Category-2 Sella Ciampigotto. With the summit 60km from the finish, vigilance was required on the drop down ahead of the final sharp climb.

HOW IT UNFOLDED / With the opening section offering gentle downhill riding, it took time for a breakaway group to muster collective speed. Eventually 20 riders forged clear including Team Sky's Salvatore Puccio, with only three teams – Lampre-Merida, Lotto Belisol and Astana – not represented.

The group built its lead along the climb of Sella Ciampigotto but, on the descent, Patrick Gretsch of Germany pressed on and opened up a gap of more than a minute on his fellow escapees and more than five minutes on a group led by Astana, shouldering the work on behalf of race leader Nibali.

Heading into the final 20km, the rest of the breakaway upped their pace with the Lithuanian Ramunas Navardauskas and Daniel Oss of Italy breaking clear and catching Gretsch. Puccio continued his strong showing with an excellent fourth place from the break, chasing the blue jersey of Stefano Pirazzi across the line. After the previous torrid day, it was a relief that Urán and Wiggins both finished safely in the peloton to hold station in the GC in third and fourth respectively.

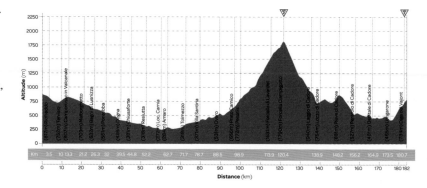

Stage 11
STATUS QUO
Wednesday 15 May / Tarvisio to Vajont, 182km

ROUTE / A day for the sprinters who could handle two sharp Category-4 climbs. The stage was otherwise anticipated to be an unofficial rest day for the GC contenders, with the final downhill 40km promising a bunch sprint.

HOW IT UNFOLDED / Relentless rain turned the short stage into a brutal ordeal. Five men formed a fugitive group and opened up a gap of three minutes plus. Their progress was hindered when all but one fell when a torrent of rainwater streamed across the road, eradicating grip.

Wiggins did not enjoy riding through a cold, a chest infection and a monsoon. He became distanced as time opened up to the surging peloton. Knees, Cataldo, Pate, Zandio, Siutsou and Puccio dropped back in a bid to peg the gap, but the team leader spent most of the stage at the back of the

pack before succumbing to the pace in the tense closing stages.

The breakaway dug deep on the finishing circuit, forcing the peloton to push hard to bridge the gap in the final 10km. This worked against Team Sky after their collective bid to help their leader. Time loss was inevitable. Stage victory went to Cavendish. Wiggins dropped to 15th overall, 5 minutes 22 seconds back on the race lead, but Urán remained safe in the bunch to retain third place.

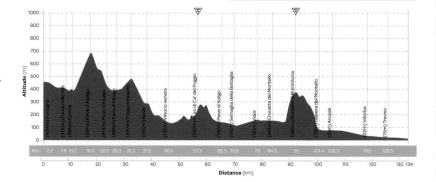

Stage 12
MONSOON MISERY
Thursday 16 May / Longarone to Treviso, 134km

ROUTE / The action moved to the north-west for another flat stage, almost twice as long as the previous day's stage. The route was flat for 150km; a Category-3 climb in the shape of Tre Cuni offered the only bump on the horizon. The last 20km undulated, with inclines that would not deter the sprinters relishing a bunch finish.

HOW IT UNFOLDED / The sun reappeared, but Team Sky headed into the longest test of the race down to eight riders after a worsening chest infection forced the withdrawal of Sir Bradley Wiggins.

Seven riders charged up the road, building up a handy advantage of 13 minutes 45 seconds. As the peloton began to step up the pace, the wind also picked up and crosswinds contributed to the reduction of that lead.

On a day that was destined to be a battle of the sprint teams versus opportunist

attackers, the undulating finale saw the race begin to split up. A series of climbs towards the finish prompted a number of late attacks but, after regrouping, the peloton soaked up the pressure. At the finish it was Cavendish who again prevailed, to claim his fourth stage win. Urán, Team Sky's new leader, was ably backed up by his team-mates to retain third overall and head back into the mountains in a strong position.

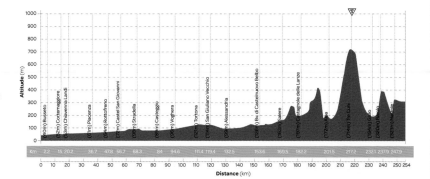

Stage 13
DOWN TO EIGHT
Friday 17 May / Busseto to Cherasco, 254km

ROUTE/ A return to the high mountains for the first of two back-to-back summit finishes before the second rest day. The route started with 70km on the flat with the riders scheduled to take on an arduous climb to the ski resort of Sestriere. An hour before the start, however, organisers cut the climb due to bad weather. The re-routed stage was lengthened by 12km but a sharp descent into the Susa valley gave tired legs a rest before the slog back up to the finish at Jafferau.

HOW IT UNFOLDED/ In freezing conditions, a breakaway group built up a lead of over 9 minutes. As the route rose up the Susa valley towards the ski resort of Bardonecchia, the peloton was able to make only small inroads into the gap.

For Team Sky, the plan was to go for the stage and set up the finish for Henao and Urán. On the final climb, a surging lead group – including Henao, Urán, and Italians Nibali and Mauro Santambrogio going head to head in the mist – eventually engulfed the breakaway.

Santambrogio pipped the win. Nibali extended his race lead. Urán clung on to third place overall after a gritty ride, crossing the line in fifth. Bonus seconds for Santambrogio bumped him to a single second behind Urán in the GC.

STAGE 14 RESULT:

Winner. Mauro Santambrogio (Ita); Vini Fantini; 04h 42' 55"
2. Vincenzo Nibali (Ita); Astana; @ same time
3. Carlos Betancur (Col); Ag2r-La Mondiale; +00' 09"

OVERALL STANDINGS:

1. Vincenzo Nibali (Ita); Astana; 57h 20' 52"
2. Cadel Evans (Aus); BMC Racing; +01' 26"
3. Rigoberto Urán (Col); Team Sky; +02' 46"

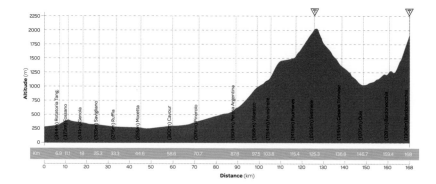

Stage 14
SNOW AND GRIT
Saturday 18 May / Cervere to Bardonecchia (Jafferau), 180km

ROUTE/ This brutal stage ended with a summit finish, and included a foray into France to tackle three categorised climbs, two of which are iconic fixtures in the Tour de France. First up was the relentless, if low-gradient, Category-1 Col du Mont Cenis, followed by the Category-2 Col du Télégraphe and the mighty Col du Galibier, where the finish line was a welcome sight after 18km of climbing at an average of 6.9 per cent.

HOW IT UNFOLDED/ The riders negotiated the first 60km without racing, taking the ascent of the Col du Mont Cenis together at a gentle pace. Racing proper kicked off just short of the summit. Six riders, including Visconti, went ahead in a bid to pick up points for the mountains classification. Reluctant to wait for the crawling peloton to catch up, they pushed on, accruing a lead of over six minutes.

The main bunch chased hard and cut the advantage to under two minutes ahead of the Col du Télégraphe climb, 31km out. Despite a flurry of attacks and deteriorating weather, Visconti dug in to secure the biggest win of his career in driving snow on the Galibier. Urán went toe-to-toe with his rivals and came in alongside the *maglia rosa* to remain in third overall, with Cadel Evans and Mauro Santambrogio crossing the line 54 seconds behind the day's winner.

STAGE 15 RESULT:

Winner. Giovanni Visconti (Ita); Movistar; 04h 40' 48"
2. Carlos Betancur (Col); Ag2r-La Mondiale; +00' 42"
3. Przemysław Niemiec (Pol); Lampre-Merida; +00' 42"

OVERALL STANDINGS:

1. Vincenzo Nibali (Ita); Astana; 62h 02' 34"
2. Cadel Evans (Aus); BMC Racing; +01' 26"
3. Rigoberto Urán (Col); Team Sky; +02' 46"

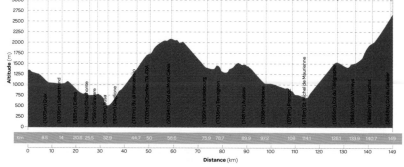

Stage 15
SUMMIT AMBITION
Sunday 19 May / Cesana Torinese to Col du Galibier (Valloire), 149km

ROUTE / The stage began with a nerve-wracking descent of the Col du Télégraphe, before the road rose back up over the Category-1 Col du Mont Cenis, which boasts its own fast, twisting descent back on to Italian soil, as the route swung east towards Turin. A flat stretch of 110 km gave the riders a breather before the Category-3 climb to Andrate, 17.5km from the finish line.

HOW IT UNFOLDED / Refreshed after their rest day, 16 riders, including Team Sky's Danny Pate, broke clear after 46km. Another six joined to form a breakaway party of 22, who built up a gap of 5 minutes. The big names hit out on the final climb. Despite the relatively short ascent to Andrate, the race exploded with a number of stinging attacks, including a move by Michele Scarponi that was quickly reined in by Nibali.

Urán slipped into a group of favourites, distancing nearest rival Santambrogio to put 2 minutes 10 seconds into the Italian at the finish. He crossed the line in 11th, alongside Nibali and Evans. The breathless finale had seen each of the contenders try to escape on the run down into Ivrea. Three riders sustained a 14-second gap in the closing kilometres, with Intxausti holding off Kangert and Niemiec in the sprint finale. GC podium places remained unchanged. Urán now held an advantage of 1 minute 7 seconds over fourth-placed Scarponi.

STAGE 16 RESULT:
Winner. Beñat Intxausti (Esp); Movistar; 05h 52' 48"
2. Tanel Kangert (Est); Astana; @ same time
3. Przemyslaw Niemiec (Pol); Lampre-Merida; @ same time
OVERALL STANDINGS:
1. Vincenzo Nibali (Ita); Astana; 67h 55' 36"
2. Cadel Evans (Aus); BMC Racing; +01' 26"
3. Rigoberto Urán (Col); Team Sky; +02' 46"

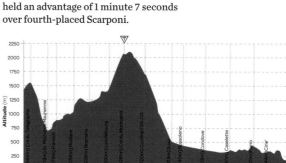

Stage 16
BREAKAWAY BRAVURA
Tuesday 21 May / Valloire to Ivrea, 238km

ROUTE / A day for the sprinters, who relished the route that passed Brescia and Verona before showing their explosive speed in the climax in Vicenza. The only obstacle was the Category-4 Crosara climb 17km from the finish.

HOW IT UNFOLDED / After a leisurely and incident-free first half of the stage, the peloton accelerated its chase of a four-man breakaway inside the last 50km. Danilo Di Luca and Giovanni Visconti had both attacked from the bunch on the lower slopes. Di Luca fell away before Visconti injected fresh pace towards the summit and descended with a 33-second lead over a reduced group of around thirty riders.

When the road levelled out, Visconti's lead fell to 22 seconds. Several riders made solo bids for glory and the gap consequently held. The Movistar man recovered from a scare when he almost

overran a corner 1.5km out and pressed on for another hard-fought success.

Salvatore Puccio continued his solid campaign by battling to sixth place. Puccio kept pace with the GC contenders on the Category-4 climb that splintered the field in the final hour of action, and then sprang to the head of the bunch to contest the sprint for second place, which was headed by Ramunas Navardauskas and Luka Mezgec. Urán maintained third place in the overall standings after rolling home alongside his nearest rivals.

STAGE 17 RESULT:
Winner. Giovanni Visconti (Ita); Movistar; 05h 15' 34"
2. Ramunas Navardauskas (Ltu); Garmin Sharp; +00' 19"
3. Luka Mezgec (Slo); Argos-Shimano; +00' 19"
OVERALL STANDINGS:
1. Vincenzo Nibali (Ita); Astana; 73h 11' 29"
2. Cadel Evans (Aus); BMC Racing; +01' 26"
3. Rigoberto Urán (Col); Team Sky; +02' 46"

Stage 17
TEAM PLAYERS
Wednesday 22 May / Caravaggio to Vicenza, 214km

BOASSON HAGEN
BOSWELL
CATALDO
DOMBROWSKI
EDMONDSON
EISEL
FROOME
HAYMAN
HENAO
KENNAUGH
KIRYIENKA
KNEES
LOPEZ
PATE
PORTE
PUCCIO
RASCH
ROWE
SIUTSOU
STANNARD
SUTTON
SWIFT
THOMAS
TIERNAN - LOCKE
URÁN
WIGGINS
ZANDIO

ROUTE/ The first of three critical days in the mountains offered GC contenders the chance to make significant gains on their rivals. The course climbed up a consistently testing gradient that reached its maximum at 10 per cent on a road riddled with hairpin bends.

HOW IT UNFOLDED/ Rigoberto Urán moved into striking distance of second place overall after an admirable performance against the clock. The Colombian secured a time good enough for sixth on the punishing uphill test to close in on second-placed Evans.

Urán led home a strong day for Team Sky, with Dario Cataldo also finishing in the top ten. His time stood up well to finish ninth, but there was no stopping Nibali. The race leader powered to victory by 58 seconds over nearest rival Samuel Sánchez and increased his advantage in

the *maglia rosa* over Evans, with Urán 10 seconds further back as the fight for the podium places intensified.

Damiano Caruso and Michele Scarponi were the next riders home, the latter taking a mere 5 seconds out of Urán on the climb as heavy rain began to fall on the leading contenders. Kanstantsin Siutsou finished just outside the top 20 as Team Sky cemented their position at the top of the team classification, taking a 5 minutes 49 seconds advantage into the remaining two mountain stages.

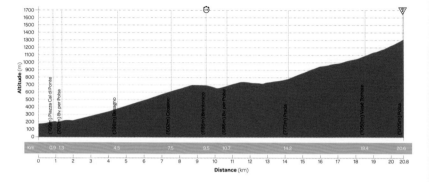

Stage 18
RACE OF TRUTH
Thursday 23 May / Mori to Polsa, 20.6km, Individual Time Trial

---

ROUTE/ The first of the second pair of back-to-back summit finishes looked tough and ready to test descending skills to the limit. The route would take the riders over three epic climbs: the Passo di Gavia, followed by the dash down to the ski resort of Bormio, then the slog back up to tackle the legendary Passo dello Stelvio, and finally the climb to the summit finish up the Val Martello.

HOW IT UNFOLDED/ Cancelled because of adverse weather conditions, with snow covering a number of the day's climbs.

The penultimate mountain test was set to run in altered form after late changes had been made to the route on the evening of Thursday 23 May. The climbs over the Passo di Gavia and the Passo dello Stelvio were removed from the route on account of the amount of snow at the summits.

Even with a revised route the weather once again conspired against the race, the two replacement climbs – the Category-2 Passo del Tonale and Category-1 Passo Castrin – both experiencing significant snowfall, and with ice also forming overnight.

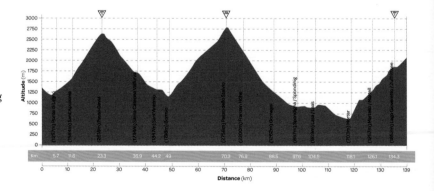

Stage 19
WHITE-OUT
Friday 24 May / Ponte di Legno to Val Martello, 160km

ROUTE / Five climbs on the agenda, with two Category-2 climbs – the Passo di Costalunga at 90km and Passo San Pellegrino at 118km – serving as warm-ups before the monstrous final 55km that kicked off with the Category-1 Passo di Giau (10.4km long, average gradient 9.1 per cent). The road dipped down to the ski resort of Cortina d'Ampezzo before rearing up to Category-2 Passo Tre Croci and the dramatic summit finish, the Tre Cime di Lavaredo.

HOW IT UNFOLDED / The route was heavily amended due to snow on high ground, with three climbs removed, but none of the keenly anticipated late drama was lost.

A four-man breakaway fractured on the lower slopes of Passo Tre Croci. Several riders attacked at the foot of the adjoining climb to the Tre Cime di Lavaredo. Three riders briefly held a minute's advantage over a depleted peloton before the pace at the front was stepped up by a determined Nibali 2.5km from the finish.

The Italian claimed victory on the spectacular summit finish to all but confirm his status as race winner, while Rigoberto Urán, valiantly supported by his team-mates, produced a sensational performance through driving snow to claim third place, and thus second place overall.

Team Sky also produced a superb display of depth, almost guaranteeing a team classification triumph.

STAGE 20 RESULT:

Winner. Vincenzo Nibali (Ita); Astana; 05h 27' 41"
2. Fabio Duarte (Col); Colombia; +00' 17"
3. Rigoberto Urán (Col); Team Sky; +00' 19"

OVERALL STANDINGS:

1. Vincenzo Nibali (Ita); Astana; 79h 23' 19"
2. Rigoberto Urán (Col); Team Sky; +04' 43"
3. Cadel Evans (Aus); BMC Racing; +05' 52"

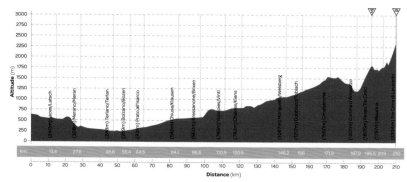

Stage 20
URÁN SECURES 2ND
Saturday 25 May / Silandro/Schlanders to Tre Cime di Lavaredo, 203km

---

ROUTE / A pan-flat route was expected to be processional for the GC contenders, allowing the sprinters to unleash their speed around seven 4.2km laps of Brescia and the dash to the finish line.

HOW IT UNFOLDED / With three of the four classifications decided, all eyes were on the sprinters' fight. Tantalisingly, Mark Cavendish had an 11-point deficit to overcome heading into the decider. Much of the day ran uncontested, celebrating the achievement of surviving three weeks of hard racing in often appalling conditions. After 85km the attacks began, but the peloton held together until the race entered the party atmosphere of Brescia.

Cavendish claimed his fifth stage victory, holding off Sacha Modolo and Elia Viviani to prise back the red points jersey at the death.

Nibali sealed race victory while Urán wrapped up a superb second place. The Colombian captured his best-ever result in a three-week Grand Tour and Team Sky's best at the Giro.

It was also a double celebration as Team Sky topped the team classification by an impressive margin of 4 minutes 29 seconds over nearest rivals Astana. Every rider had contributed to the superb result.

The young rider's white jersey was secured by Carlos Betancur; Stefano Pirazzi had already claimed the mountains classification.

STAGE 21 RESULT:

Winner. Mark Cavendish (GB); Omega Pharma-Quick Step; 05h 30' 09"
2. Sacha Modolo (Ita); Bardiani Valvole; @ same time
3. Elia Viviani (Ita); Cannondale; @ same time

OVERALL STANDINGS:

1. Vincenzo Nibali (Ita); Astana; 84h 53' 28"
2. Rigoberto Urán (Col); Team Sky; +04' 43"
3. Cadel Evans (Aus); BMC Racing; +05' 52"

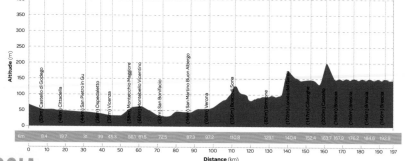

Stage 21
CHAMPAGNE IN BRESCIA
Sunday 26 May / Riese Pio X to Brescia, 197km

The first time I registered the Tour de France as a huge event was in 2002 when I was a teenager, 17 years old, and living in a boarding house at my school, St John's College, Johannesburg. Growing up in Kenya, I hadn't been exposed to the Tour. I don't think many people had satellite television and I can't recall seeing footage of the race. That first Tour I followed on television in South Africa really captured my imagination. The sight of Lance Armstrong and a young Ivan Basso fighting it out in the mountains coincided with my own developing interest in cycling.

Five years later, I withdrew from university two years into an economics degree to turn professional and started road racing in South Africa, specialising as a climber. I made my Grand Tour début in the 2008 Tour de France, becoming the first-ever participant from Kenya to start the event, and finishing 84th overall and 11th in the young rider classification, which was dominated by Andy Schleck and Vincenzo Nibali. At that point, the idea of winning the Tour – or wearing the iconic yellow jersey – was a far-off dream, but I remember thinking how much I would love to develop enough to win it and wondering if it were possible.

It wasn't until the Vuelta a España in 2011 – where I finished second overall for Team Sky – that I realised I was able to compete at the highest level and that my dream could become a reality. In terms of breakthroughs and milestones, I earned my first Grand Tour stage win in the Vuelta; and by finishing as overall runner-up, I also equalled Robert Millar's record for securing the highest finish by a British rider in a Grand Tour.

In 2012 I suffered a lot of hiccups during the winter and early-season races, with illnesses and accidents. It wasn't plain sailing, but as I stood on the second step of the Tour de France podium in Paris, I became determined to return the following year in the leadership position. When Team Sky gave me that role, I focused hard on establishing my own brand of leadership style and enjoyed the collaboration with team-mates, management and behind-the-scenes staff. Early on in the 2013 season I wore yellow jerseys in other races – the Critérium International in March, the Tour de Romandie in April, the Critérium du Dauphiné in June. We had a string of wins that just seemed to gain momentum.

All the time I was looking ahead to the Tour de France, visualising certain mountain-top finishes, mentally undertaking some of the climbs, imagining what could happen. But in none of my dreams was it the epic journey it turned out to be . . .

THE STORY OF THE TOUR
INTRODUCTION BY CHRIS FROOME

STAGE 1 / p.120

STAGE 2 / p.126

STAGE 3 / p.130

STAGE 7 / p.144

STAGE 8 / p.146

STAGE 9 / p.152

STAGE 13 / p.170

STAGE 14 / p.172

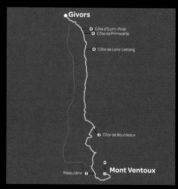

STAGE 15 / p.174

THE TOUR ROUTE

STAGE 4 / p.134

STAGE 5 / p.138

STAGE 6 / p.140

Saint-Malo
Côte de Dinan ⑤
Vannes
Saint-Gildas-des-Bois

STAGE 10 / p.158

Avranches
Mont Saint-Michel

STAGE 11 / p.160

Fougères
Rennes
Savigné-Sur-Lathan ⑤
Nantes
Tours

STAGE 12 / p.166

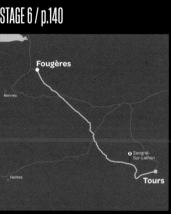

Col de Manse ②
Veynes
Gap
Vaison-La-Romaine
Côte de la ③
Montagne de Bluye
Col de Macuègne ②

STAGE 16 / p.180

Côte de Réallon ②
Côte de Puy-Sanières ③
Chorges
Embrun

STAGE 17 / p.184

Col de Sarenne
Alpe-D'Huez 2
Col d'Ornon
Bourg-d'Oisans
Rampe du Motty ③
Col de Manse ②

STAGE 18 / p.186

Le Grand-Bornand
Col de la Croix Fry ⑦
Col de l'Épine ⑦
Col de Tamié
Albertville
Col de la Madeleine ②
Grenoble
Col du Glandon ②
Bourg-d'Oisans

STAGE 19 / p.190

Annecy
Annecy-Semnoz
Côte de Puget
Col de Leschaux
Le Châtelard
Mont Revard
Côte d'Allon-le-Vieux
Col des Prés

STAGE 20 / p.192

Paris Champs-Élysées
Versailles
Côte de Châteaufort ④
Côte de Saint-Rémy-lès-Chevreuse ④

STAGE 21 / p.194

A few centuries ago a 'Grand Tour' meant a cultural trip around Europe undertaken by young men as a rite of passage. In the same spirit, there was no doubt that the 2013 Tour de France, the most prestigious of cycling's Grand Tours, would be an exacting and enriching experience for all its participants – not just defending champions, Team Sky.

For riders seeking to make an impact, the 100th edition of the race promised much by association, with its first-time *Grand Départ* on the island of Corsica, birthplace of Napoleon Bonaparte and Christopher Columbus. As the only region of France never previously traversed by the race, and as the southernmost starting point in the Tour's history, the mountainous Corsican stages seemed to promise breakthroughs and new horizons for young riders entering their prime in a transitional period for cycling.

The reality of Grand Tour racing meant that the stages from Porto-Vecchio to Bastia, and on to Ajaccio and subsequently Calvi, would also conjure crashes and mishaps, first-week nerves and fretfulness. How would it play out for Team Sky? For Chris Froome, aiming to live up to his status as pre-race favourite? For Richie Porte, Edvald Boasson Hagen and Kanstantsin Siutsou, returning as members of the victorious 2012 team with memories good and bad? (Siutsou had broken his leg early in Sir Bradley Wiggins's crusade.) For David López and Geraint Thomas, notching up their third and fourth Tours de France respectively? For Vasili Kiryienka in his second, and Ian Stannard and Peter Kennaugh, both making their début quest for the yellow jersey? On the eve of the race, a team insider noticed a bright yellow butterfly flutter about, then settle above the row of Sky's black Pinarello bikes. A good omen?

'I'm super-excited,' said Stannard. 'You always hear about how massive the Tour is and how fast and stressful the racing is. I'm just keen to get going. It's going to be hard riding for Froomey, given that he's the overwhelming favourite. The other teams will all be looking to put one over on us, but we've got big ambitions of our own. We're ready to race.' Boasson Hagen, who popped a crowd-pleasing wheelie en route to the start, also expressed excitement. 'It gives us extra confidence to see that Froomey is up there, in the mix,' he said. 'It's very motivating to know he is counting on help from all of us.'

In 2012 Wiggins became the first British rider to win the Tour, by gaining substantial margins in the time trials and then defending his lead. In 2013, with a team leader

STAGE 1

who excels at climbing, the plan was to go out and win it in the mountains. 'Last year felt very controlled,' said team principal Sir Dave Brailsford. 'This year, instead of thinking it was our title to defend, we wanted to go out to try and win it a second time, starting from zero. That seemed a more positive way of looking at it. We knew the other teams would go very much on the attack and take the race to us in a more aggressive way than in the previous edition. Collectively, with strength in numbers, they would concertedly try to thwart us.'

In the absence of Wiggins, Froome was wearing the coveted number '1'. Over 21 days, he would have to dominate a field that included the likes of Alberto Contador, Alejandro Valverde and Cadel Evans to earn the right to finish as number '1' when the centenary spectacular concluded at dusk in Paris. 'I couldn't get going soon enough,' he recalled. 'Those two weeks, waiting, waiting, were the hardest. You taper off training, you have time on your hands . . . It's like tempting something to go wrong.'

As press officer, Dario Cioni – a former rider who in Sky's first year, 2010, registered the team's highest GT finish – was a weather-vane for gauging external expectation. 'The pressure was much greater this summer because we had done it with Brad and we were returning to try to win it with a different rider, Chris. It was also a younger team. The British guys, Peter and Ian, didn't know what to expect.'

'In the meeting before the Tour, I wanted to emphasise to young riders like Peter and Ian that when you're away for four weeks, it's important to look after yourself,' said *directeur sportif* Nicolas Portal. 'Catnap when you can. Don't waste time on Facebook and Twitter. Find some quiet time for yourself. Don't forget your first job is to be ready in the morning to race, to do yourself justice. In the Tour, every day, there are lots of media, fans, people chanting, encouraging, pushing for autographs. For the first few days, it is very, very hard.'

As Brailsford says of the best-intentioned plans, sometimes life gets in the way. On 29 June 2013, all those weeks of intense training in Tenerife, of riding up and down volcanoes, of testing form and forging team spirit at the Tour of Oman, Critérium International, Tour de Romandie and Critérium du Dauphiné were nearly scuppered when a concrete bollard got in the way of Chris Froome's front wheel as he was warming up in the neutralised zone. 'The road narrowed, I was in the wrong place at the wrong time,' he said. 'I was fine, but annoyed because I knew people would think it was because I was nervous . . . and I wasn't.'

'It was a fright hearing that the first guy down of 200-plus competitors was the guy wearing number "1" on his jersey,' remembered team doctor Alan Farrell, who was about to face his busiest day of the entire Tour.

Froome was quickly up, with a grazed right knee to indicate battle had commenced. And what a fray it was. As the stage action neared conclusion, the Orica-GreenEDGE bus became wedged under the overhead gantry, blocking the finish line. Race radio first brought forward the finish by three kilometres, then switched it back as the bus was dislodged, resulting in carnage. Stannard and Thomas crashed, as did Peter Sagan and Contador; pre-stage favourite Mark Cavendish was held up. Chaos ensured a reduced bunch headed into Bastia with Marcel Kittel claiming the first yellow jersey. 'The bus! No one knew what was going on,' recalled Cioni, while Portal remembers feeling it was too early in the campaign to be saying, 'Guys, swap plans *again*!'

Five hours earlier, the peloton was a collective mass of supremely fit athletes. Now world time-trial champion Tony Martin was en route to hospital, having lost consciousness twice, Stannard had incurred a back injury and Thomas, the man Froome valued as his indomitable road captain, was in agony with a fractured pelvis. 'It was one of the first times I can remember where I couldn't get up straight away,' recalled Thomas, who is universally known as 'G'. 'Even when I'd ruptured my spleen in 2005, it was nothing like as painful. If it had been any other race I would have gone home, but the Tour is the World Cup of cycling and I was determined to stick around to do the job for Chris.'

Among the ripped Lycra, raw skin and developing bruises, Froome considered his own mishap fortunate. 'If that's the only pressure I have this Tour, I'll take that. It's been quite a warning. I don't think any of us thought it would be plain sailing today, but there were some pretty brutal crashes – a reminder that this Tour is about much more than having the form and being here. It's about staying out of trouble. I felt guys crashing all around me . . . All I could hear was the sound of breaking bikes and shoes scraping on the road.'

STAGE 2

'Everyone suffers from nerves in the first week of the Tour but to almost lose two riders on the first day left us a bit worried,' said Servais Knaven, Portal's fellow *directeur sportif*. 'G was our road captain. We needed someone who takes the lead on behalf of Chris on the road, otherwise Chris has too much thinking to do as well as riding. It was big blow to see G in so much pain.'

The double Olympic champion was in excruciating pain, but was determined to carry on. 'When I got to the bus that morning, I could see him struggling to get on and off the bike,' said Cioni. 'But from that moment on, G showed everyone who G is.'

Thanks to a combination of Thomas's innate fighting spirit, Team Sky's excellent injury-assessment procedures and Rod Ellingworth's expectation-management, G remained on the road. 'It felt like an eternity when I was out there for those 156 kilometres. Those first 10ks were by far the hardest time I have ever had on a bike. There were quite a few roundabouts and, having to accelerate out of those, I found that I just couldn't keep up with the lead group. I couldn't get out of the saddle, couldn't generate any power in my left leg. I was worried, thinking that I would struggle to finish within the time limit. But I was never going to stop.'

Thomas's mum, watching from home, texted him: 'It's OK. You're allowed to retire.' But the doctors had diagnosed his injury as a 'stable fracture' and considered he'd do himself no further harm by continuing to ride his bike. 'That

was great to hear. The only thing holding me back was the pain.' And his mother? 'She convinced herself that I was in safe hands. In the end the support from home was crucial. At the toughest moments I would look at all the Welsh flags by the roadside and realise that I had to carry on.'

Ellingworth, team performance manager, was quick to rally Thomas's spirits with practical guidance. 'My day-to-day job is to make sure the performance of the team is on track. I'm ready to pinpoint any potential hurdle or issue – whether it's the heat, a particular climb or a technical section of road. I gather information and present it to the *directeurs sportifs*. I also make sure the other side of the team's presence on the Tour – the media, VIPs, hospitality – doesn't impact on performance. I try to keep everything organised so that the lads can concentrate on doing their jobs and I can keep a load of additional stuff off the *DS*s [*directeurs sportifs*]. I hold it together.'

He also knows the riders well. Having played a key role in nurturing a golden generation of British cyclists before joining Team Sky as race coach in 2010, Ellingworth has a mentor-like approach in helping each individual eke out their best performance. 'During a Grand Tour, I know how to keep their spirits up when they have a bad crash. Geraint needed help after his fall in terms of realigning his performance expectations. He had come in, in perfect condition, determined to show what he could do in the mountains, but now he had a fractured pelvis. From that day on, my aim was to help him get through the race to the end, feeling good about his contribution.'

The peloton wound south-west across Corsica's mountainous spine. 'I remember in the first 20 to 30 kilometres when everyone was attacking, and the pace was high, wondering if G could hang on,' Froome recalls. 'That day was the real danger point.' In glorious sunshine, Team Sky hit the front on the early climbs to position Froome so that on the final ascent he was able to ride clear of the bunch, 12 kilometres from the finish in Ajaccio. Having followed Richie Porte up the first 700 metres of the 1km climb, Froome took his rivals by surprise with a quick turn of speed. 'The descent was tricky so, on the front with Richie, I thought it might be a good time to push on a bit, get ahead, take the descent at my own pace and stay out of trouble. It's good to keep people on their toes!'

The day also gave an early indication of Froome's style of leadership, the caring way in which he looked out for his team. Stannard and Thomas came home safely, 195th and 196th respectively, earning the respect of their team principal as guys who are natural fighters and who don't roll over when the going gets tough. G was now *the* big story and Froome, giving interviews as he warmed down on the turbo, noticed him pinned against the bus by a throng of microphones and cameras. With a thumbs up to Siutsou and Kennaugh as they walked past, Froome wound up his media commitments, went over to stand alongside Thomas and took over the spotlight to allow G to retreat and recover.

After two days on fairly generous stretches of asphalt, the road looked trickier on the final day on Corsica. The course designer had said with pride that it included 'not a metre of flat'. As well as an ever-changing gradient, the route wiggled relentlessly; team members sitting in the back seat of the cars were in for a nauseating ride. For the riders, the reward for surviving the rollercoaster route was a relentless run to a sprint finish over even narrower, winding roads. On days like this, which would require red-alert vigilance, the relationship between team leader and *directeur sportif* comes into its own. At 34, Nicolas Portal was the youngest *DS* at the race. The business of divulging information, tactical suggestions, cautions, reassurance and encouragement over the radio works only with supreme trust and mutual confidence. With Portal and Froome, this relationship stems from their year as team-mates when both joined Team Sky as riders in 2010.

'I didn't speak English when I first met him but I still found Chris to be very open,' says Portal. 'He's a true person, a genuine guy. Inside the team he's very bright, charismatic. He knows what he wants to do. To be that young and talented would give some people a big ego, but Chris is just everyone's friend. He doesn't put up barriers. Everyone wants to work to support him. He's a guy who likes discussing things openly. He might ask me, "Nico, is this a good plan?" It's mutual collaboration with him. That creates a climate where there's a lot of trust. Working with Chris, you feel good, you feel respected and you're in a position of confidence. On the first morning in Corsica, for example, he confided to me that he was feeling a bit stressed. He thought maybe it was because it was the first time he'd been a leader at the Tour. At the end of the first stage – despite all the chaos – I could see all that pressure had come off him.

'Working with him now that I am a *DS* is the same as when I was a rider: very straightforward. His biggest quality, apart from having an extraordinary physique, is that he's not consumed by star attitude or by the scale of the event he's riding; he's polite, says thanks to everyone, and he doesn't have a big head. That attitude is important. When you're travelling close together for four weeks – staff and riders – it's easier for everyone to give 100 per cent if you're all working for a nice leader. If you're working for someone with a huge ego, it's more like 99 per cent. For a cyclist, the Tour is like the World Cup or the Olympics. It's a long race, with all the tension you'd expect as it pans out, but everyone was determined to give 100 per cent for Chris.'

It has been a parallel rise to responsibility for Froome and Portal as team leader and *DS* respectively. 'Chris was told he'd be leader last winter, so he knew how to prepare for the long build-up season. He'd have to find his own way to take on that role. Every team leader's personality is different. We'd say, "You're Chris Froome. We need to lead the team your way." The plan in the build-up was to learn

STAGE 3

a lot about how we'd work together, how we'd collaborate over the radio, how we'd plan to win the race. Everything we did was thinking ahead to seven months into the future – to the Tour. Every race he was a big hit against all the GC contenders – Contador, Valverde, Rodríguez, Evans. It was very important for the team to try to win all these races. Everything had to be right. There was BIG pressure in the races, learning on our way, but every race was productive for the full team. Ultimately, we realised there was a lot of confidence, good attitude and self-belief.'

When Brailsford asked Portal to be lead *DS* for the races up to and including the Tour, the Frenchman was initially flummoxed. I said: 'Responsible for a Grand Tour and Chris?! Are you sure?! My English is not so good! But the fact that I had all the management behind me as support – Dave, Rod and so on – I knew they would make sure I could do it well. The pressure for me was to make sure I felt confident enough. In the days before a Grand Tour, everyone's nervous, but on the first morning, talking through the stage profile, the tactics and strategies with the riders, I felt calm. When it was over, and they'd filed off the bus, then I felt the pressure of seeing what might happen. Twenty-one new teams lining up – we don't know who they all are! The dynamic of a big event like the Tour is hard to anticipate.'

On the day, as feared, attacks fired off over the top of the spectacular final climb – the Col de Marsolino – with the Frenchman Sylvain Chavanel driving a four-man move that included the polka dot jersey of his compatriot Pierre Rolland. The pace on this toughest of stages sunk many a sprinter's hopes of glory. Riding hard, the reduced peloton was able to fend off the move to set up a sprint in which the Australian Simon Gerrans timed his bike throw perfectly to better the Slovak star Peter Sagan. Froome finished safely, escorted to the finish line by Porte and Boasson Hagen. The Norwegian retained Team Sky's highest position in the general classification – fifth place – with Froome and Porte 15th and 24th respectively, all one second behind the yellow jersey of the Belgian Jan Bakelants.

It was good to see Boasson Hagen and Porte in fine fettle, displaying the strength in depth of Froome's support squad. 'It takes a few days to get the legs going in a Grand Tour, but I was feeling quite good,' said the Norwegian. 'I managed to get over the last mountain in a good position, but it was hard to do anything in the last sprint because of hammering it on the last climb.' With Geraint Thomas clinging on to the back of the peloton, every Team Sky rider had come home safely, ready for the plane transfer to Nice – with everything still to play for on a tantalisingly even field.

For the rest of the Tour circus, it was 'the night of the living dead' as they took the night ferry to the Côte d'Azur, arriving zombie-like to face the team time trial.

STAGE 4

For spectators, an individual time trial most stirs those with trainspotterish tendencies. A team time trial, on the other hand, is one of the sport's most accessible visual thrills. The sight of a team of world-class cyclists, tucked into aerodynamic crouches, riding full pelt as a unit, with individuals rotating in turns to take the pull on the front, is quite something – like the Red Arrows on wheels, glorious synchronicity powered by collective drive and vision.

It's also famously stressful. No rider wants to let his team-mates down. No rider wants to undertake the sprint feeling under par. As any rider will tell you, 'If you're not 100 per cent, it's agony, because you're at full gas the whole distance.' A team's time is taken as the fifth rider crosses the line, so the teams preparing to rocket in formation around the glorious beach-front circuit in Nice would be relying on a nucleus of strong all-rounders who weren't feeling any ill effects after three tough days in Corsica . . .

For Team Sky, carrying two injured riders in Thomas and Stannard, the dynamic was therefore more 'interesting' than usual, according to Boasson Hagen, Team Sky's highest-placed rider and thus potentially in line to take the yellow jersey. 'As a team we had to be extremely focused in a different way. With G and Ian both in a lot of pain, I was extra nervous for them . . . as well as for myself and the team.'

'When we came to the team time trial, G would've obviously been one of our strongest riders,' said Brailsford.

'It was a real concern that morning, not just that he couldn't sprint, but that he couldn't accelerate quickly enough. If he was left off the back at the start, we might lose him for the rest of the Tour. So we broke the route down and told him he had 700 metres from the middle of Nice to the Promenade des Anglais to go really hard and get himself on the back of the line. He really got himself up for it, went for it on those 700 metres and hung on the back. Then it was about keeping in contact with the team. Those first three minutes were his big objective. Not only did he do that – after another three minutes he then started going through, taking turns, and pulling as strong as anyone else. It was incredible to see, a phenomenal performance.'

Fans could tell from Thomas's Twitter presence that he was in good spirits before Team Sky's 2.51pm start. 'Thanks for all the messages guys, much appreciated!!! Even the dope control guys came to wish me well, and take my urine . . .'

If he hung on to the back of the train and finished no further than 10 per cent adrift of the team's time, all would be well. 'We knew it was going to be hard to manage the logistics because we couldn't afford to start slowly to make sure G could follow,' recalls Portal. 'You need to be full gas from the off. It was going to be quite tricky because G could only sit on his saddle and pedal as hard as he could. His pain wouldn't allow him to stand up to accelerate. He would have to be right on it, and accurate. It was very high pressure, the first day of the Tour on mainland France, the centenary edition, people watching from every rooftop.'

Having won the team time trial at the Giro d'Italia – their first in a Grand Tour – Team Sky were tipped to win the Nice shootout. Under the circumstances, finishing third and featuring on the podium was a terrific result. The valiant Thomas clung on until just over a kilometre to go. 'It wasn't too bad. It's over so quick,' he quipped. 'It's tougher on the road stages. I just wanted to get stuck in for the boys.'

'It was a breathtaking effort all round and filled the team with confidence and pride,' said Brailsford. 'We knew after that, that we were very close to taking the yellow jersey.' Just three seconds faster and the amiable Boasson Hagen could have been in the iconic race leader's jersey. 'It wasn't the goal to get it, but I'd have been very happy to wear it!' he said.

For Chris Froome, the result left his campaign perfectly poised. Three more days to survive on the flat, then the mountains. 'We're happy. We tried to win it, but if we were in yellow, it would mean over the next couple of predominantly flat stages we'd have to be on the front, possibly expending all that effort on defending just a few seconds, which would be a bit unnecessary,' he said. 'The important thing is I feel good. I was able to do longer pulls on the front. I'm feeling like I'm really coming into some good form ready for the mountains.'

The team time trial had settled anxieties after the setbacks of the opening day. It was back to business as usual, taking stock of the standings, adapting plans to ensure that Froome stayed out of trouble, as the next three stages were set to conclude with frenetic sprints into Marseilles, Montpellier and Albi respectively. One priority was to consider who would help contribute to Thomas's road-captain duties while he recovered.

'Normally, the captain would be at the front for the first 20 to 25 kilometres, assessing the breakaways, moving around the bunch, protecting Chris,' said Portal. 'The role requires the ability to do big accelerations. With G on the back bench, we needed to rely on someone else to read the moves and be vocal. I talked sometimes to Edvald – experienced, calm, but quiet – and sometimes to Peter Kennaugh.'

Portal and Servais Knaven think through 1,000 different scenarios every morning – 'and scenario number 1,001 always crops up on the day,' laughs the Dutchman in charge of the second team car. On one stretch of the road from Cagnes-sur-Mer to Marseilles, tacks scattered across the surface was the scenario that threatened to keep both cars busy sorting out punctures. After Porte and Thomas experienced flat tyres, the mechanics found tacks embedded in the rubber. The incident served as an uneasy reminder of how vulnerable riders are to random behaviour from spectators. 'It was a bit of a hostile crowd this year,' says Porte. 'Tacks are not a big deal when you're not going fast, but if you're going at speed it's not just sabotage but attempted manslaughter. It's that serious.'

Having raised the concern with organisers, Portal was thankful that no race-threatening damage was done. 'The most important thing I learnt from my teacher, Sean Yates [the former Team Sky *DS* who had retired the previous year], is to stay calm and be practical when situations like that arise,' he said. 'OK, this has happened. Now I need to find the solution. You can't start to worry or panic or show emotion because then stress starts.'

Boasson Hagen was relishing being in the thick of the action and sniffing after a career third Tour stage win. Without the benefit of a lead-out train, he produced tremendous pace to finish second in the sprint, just edged out by Mark Cavendish, but beating the likes of André Greipel, Peter Sagan, Marcel Kittel and John Degenkolb.

Froome was happy to tick off another day. 'Our game-plan continues to be to stay near the front and out of trouble – to try and keep ahead of most of the problems – but it seems most of the crashes these days are at the front so you have to stay awake at all times.'

STAGE 5

STAGE 6

On a hot, tense, windy day in Provence, Daryl Impey, Chris Froome's former training partner, took the yellow jersey, thus becoming the first South African to wear the Tour de France leader's iconic *maillot jaune*. 'If you'd ever told me I'd get to experience this, I'd have said you were lying,' Impey declared. 'This is a dream come true, a magical moment, a big day for South Africa, for African cycling.'

Impey's achievement was an act of consolidation in terms of his home nation's cycling heritage. For, six years earlier, it was also on a sprint stage concluding in Montpellier that Robbie Hunter had become the first South African to win a stage of the Tour. Those who enjoy finding some form of validity in connections such as that between Hunter and Impey were tempted to extend the run of coincidences and ponder whether Froome might prove to be the second history-maker out of Africa on this 2013 edition of the race. To see a close friend achieve a goal he had always thought unattainable helped reduce the mystique of the Tour's ultimate prize, adding an emotional momentum to the physiological and statistical evidence that showed Froome had the athleticism, stamina and form to secure an overall win.

The fact that Impey inherited the yellow jersey from his team-mate Simon Gerrans, too, emphasised the rewarding fellowship of team unity. 'It really was a cool story in a lot of ways – from getting the yellow jersey from Simon to it being a monumental thing for African cycling,' says Froome. 'Daryl had helped Simon get into the yellow jersey a few days before and the roles reversed a couple of days later. For me, seeing guys I am really familiar with wearing the yellow jersey definitely made the prospect of me winning it become more realistic.'

With the Mistral threatening to blow across the peloton on its progression from Aix-en-Provence to Montpellier, Froome relied on the support and protection of his team-mates. 'Chris knows what he wants to do, but he knows how to listen. He likes to hear a bit of everybody's views and then put his cards on the table, saying, OK, we will do this and this and this,' says Portal. 'He's the kind of leader who takes decisions during the race. He talks a lot with me on the radio. It's important that everyone keeps communicating – not just him talking to me, but him keeping in touch with the other riders in the team as well.'

When crosswinds blow across the bunch, riders seeking shelter end up in an echelon that stretches diagonally across the road. This formation harshly minimises the numbers who can stay in the line of protection without going off the road, thus causing the dreaded wind-induced splinters in the peloton. So, on a day of peloton splinters and hustling sprinters, Froome was pleased to count on the help he received from the ever-tenacious Porte, the strong and versatile Boasson Hagen, the powerfully consistent Belorussians Vasili Kiryienka

and Kanstantsin Siutsou, the tirelessly reliable David López, Peter Kennaugh and big-hearted Ian Stannard, while Geraint Thomas continued to endure personal pain to contribute to the Team Sky effort.

'It was very nervous out there but the wind seemed to be swirling over the riders' heads,' said Portal. 'It didn't actually affect them as much as we thought it would. That's why everything stayed together, but the pace was kept so high because everyone wanted to be near the front if it did pick up. Our goal was to stay focused and we did that. We committed to riding as near to the front as we could and the boys did a good job for Froomey. David and Kosta did the work early on, and then Richie and Kiry took over. Pete, Ian and G also chipped in as the stage wore on. G's morale was improving – along with his condition – every day, and that was pleasing to see. Those guys were all working brilliantly as a unit out there, and you can't ask for any more than that.'

Boasson Hagen sat out the sprint, but moved up to second place in the general classification, which was a nice bonus. Froome rolled home alongside the other general classification contenders in 18th position and was relieved to get another potentially dangerous day in the bag. 'It's been a stressful week so far, but good at the same time,' he said with his customary calm demeanour. 'On the whole we've come through it well as a team and we're sitting in a really good position now heading into the Pyrenees. I'm definitely looking forward to getting into the harder climbs now. It's been quite nerve-wracking on the flats. Everyone's really close on the general classification and everyone's fighting for position, but hopefully once we hit the climbs it's going to open up a little bit more and the race will calm down a bit.

'There was a lot of pushing and shoving today. I can understand the sprinters wanting a clean sprint – they don't want GC riders in their way – but I can also see it from the GC riders' point of view. We want to stay up there and fight for those positions if there's the threat of losing seconds in the final like what happened today. I'm very happy with where we are, though. We're in a great position and I'm really pleased with the team I've got around me, both on and off the bike, so I'm looking forward to getting stuck into next week.'

Looking beyond the view from inside the Team Sky bubble, the results of the sixth stage of the Tour showed cycling to be a truly global sport. Nine countries were represented in the top ten of the overall standings: South Africa, Norway, Australia (twice), Switzerland, France, Great Britain, Poland, the Czech Republic and Ireland. Each of the jerseys was held by a different nationality, from Impey in yellow to the Slovak Peter Sagan in green, the Frenchman Rolland in polka dot and the Pole Michal Kwiatkowski in white.

Unlike the Giro, where conditions deteriorated day by day, the Tour was blessed with blue skies and scorching sunshine. 'During the preparation races the weather in Europe had been more like winter. Taking on lots of fluids had not been so important. Suddenly, the temperatures were extremely hot and we had to chase the riders to make sure everyone was eating and drinking enough,' said Servais Knaven. 'By the end of the first week, we were discovering how important it was to be spot on with nutrition and rehydration drinks.'

Food is fuel for elite athletes, but Søren Kristiansen, the team chef, believes that it should be restorative psychologically as well as physically. 'I keep it interesting for the riders, playing with colour, texture and flavours on the plate. You eat with your eyes, so I use bright colours such as fresh mango, raw spinach, aubergine, squash and red cabbage. I marinate chicken with ginger, lime, mint, basil, coriander; or serve fresh tuna with peaches, lemon, melon, tomato and avocado.' To initially kick-start the riders' digestive systems at dinner, Søren might serve a big salad full of things that need to be chewed well. Then, to ease the workload on a rider's stomach, he uses vegetable purees and juices to ensure they get the right nutrients and rehydration. 'I talk almost daily to Nigel Mitchell, the team nutritionist. If we're going into the mountains, the riders need to fill up a bit more, but we serve only white meat and fish because they're easier to digest. Red meat requires the body to work harder and use up more energy to process. The idea is, "If I'm smiling inside my body, my legs are working better!"'

Søren's daily spells in the kitchen with his precious knives and personal chopping board are equivalent to the riders' on their bikes. In between, he has to factor in logistics, travel and equipment issues as well as sorting out his shopping and kitchen territory. He emails each hotel eight days in advance with ingredient requests and pops out to local markets to satisfy his desire to find the freshest fish and top-quality chicken. 'I always play it safe. It's just me, my responsibility. I only have two hands and even if I'm only cooking for nine riders, that's the equivalent of feeding 18 normal people. I use the hotel kitchens, a different one almost every night; the best thing is when the kitchen chef likes cycling. If he asks me what football team I support, I always say the wrong one! I bring my own knives, induction plates, pots, pans and juicer. In my car I have fridges and ten boxes full of gluten- and sugar-free ingredients.'

In a team comprising many nationalities, the riders' wish-lists can vary from the Brits wanting Yorkshire pudding to the Colombian clamour for banana cake. 'All those national tastes are not easy to satisfy. We compromise with mainly Mediterranean influences. We also have a policy, "If you're not happy, say it. If you are happy, also say it!"'

STAGE 7

STAGE 8

There it loomed: the Pyrenean ski resort of Ax 3 Domaines, the first big GC-shaking summit finish and the highest point of the centenary Tour. While plenty of riders considered the final pair of climbs 'daunting', one Christopher Froome – as the French had taken to calling him – considered them positively inviting. 'For me, arriving in the mountains signifies you've reached the certain point you need to get to before you can go for your goal,' he said, sounding like a mountaineer reaching base camp on Mount Everest.

'All our training has been tailored towards being good in the mountains. In the first seven days of a Grand Tour, there's so much scope for things to go wrong and catch you out. When you reach the mountains, you think, "It's now just up to my legs." If you're confident in your training, your preparation, it's a good place to arrive at. I was looking forward to tackling Ax 3 Domaines. As the first mountain-top finish, it represented the first genuine battle for me against my rivals. I knew it would definitely be a fight on the climb, but it was here we would see what everyone had come to the Tour with.' Relief at reaching higher altitudes extended throughout the team. Dave Brailsford suggested the day represented 'a bit of sparring, the first round in a bout' for Froome. 'I wouldn't say we're going for yellow. We have to be flexible and adapt our tactics,' he said. 'But if it happens, it happens.'

It happened all right. As Servais Knaven said: 'Chris took it on and there was no looking back.' Blowing the race to pieces, Froome won his first stage victory of the 2013 Tour and claimed the yellow jersey from his former training partner and good friend, Daryl Impey, becoming the sixth Briton ever to wear the *maillot jaune*. The way in which this masterly display of strength unfolded was textbook dominance from Team Sky. A precisely executed Sky train launched him to the point where one last insuppressible 5km burst obliterated his tiring rivals.

Not only did the team leader win the stage, but his super-*domestique* Richie Porte came second, leaving the pair in first and second place overall. It was a deeply satisfying scenario for the team management, who had pinpointed the exact place to attack in order to take most time out of Froome's GC opponents. Former Tour de France champions Alberto Contador, Andy Schleck and Cadel Evans all suffered significant blows finishing behind Froome by 1 minute 46 seconds, 3 minutes 35 seconds and 4 minutes 14 seconds respectively.

Gentle pastoral scenes disguised the sharpest of aggressive plans. Under blue skies, with sunshine playing on emerald Pyrenean slopes, the peloton allowed four

men – including Christophe Riblon, a winner on this section three years ago – to forge ahead, while Team Sky and Orica-GreenEDGE combined at the front to maintain a businesslike pace. Geraint Thomas, riding with more ease by the day, swapped off in rotation with the team of outgoing race leader Impey. After the intermediate sprint, won by André Greipel, the GC teams rallied ahead of the 15.3km Pailhères ascent. Rival trains formed. Riblon pushed onwards. Robert Gesink and Thomas Voeckler attacked before the diminutive, nimble figure of Nairo Quintana fired clear to crest the climb first. The peloton followed just over a minute later, with a concerted turn from each and every member of Team Sky, led by Richie Porte and Peter Kennaugh, who efficiently smothered attack after attack.

'Everyone in Sky or GB cycling knows how good Peter Kennaugh is,' said Richie Porte. 'That was the day the world saw his talent. It's difficult to give one team-mate credit when everyone was brilliant, but on Ax 3 Domaines he showed who and what he was. I remember we were on a fast, technical descent, Peter, Chris and I. I looked at my speedo and saw 93 km/h – on not very good roads. Peter led the tempo into the climb. He then did another great pull and then it was just Chris and I. Chris looked at me and said, "There's nobody left!" And that was that. Chris went, and for me it was strange . . . I was able to finish second, 17 seconds ahead of Valverde, and move up to second on the GC. It was fantastic, the same scenario as with Brad last year.'

With Movistar's young Colombian Quintana overhauled on the final Category-1 ramps, Froome and Porte had set out their stall for how they intended to race in the mountains – accelerating in emphatic trademark climbing style to lead home a Team Sky one–two. Froome's stunning attack in the final 5km rewarded him with a 51-second lead over his team-mate in the yellow jersey standings.

'That was a joyful moment,' said Knaven. 'Froomey had been waiting for that day for more than a year. He went full gas in the last 5km, not waiting for anyone else. It was a dream way to take yellow, a mountain-top finish.'

'This is incredible. We have worked for months to be in this position,' said Froome. 'Once I pulled clear of the other guys I knew I had to go into almost time-trial mode to take the biggest advantage possible in the stage. I definitely wasn't holding anything back. This is the Tour de France. Every second counts. There's a long way to Paris still, but this is a dream come true for me. I've been in a few leaders' jerseys this year but nothing compares to this.'

The outstanding performance led immediately to Froome being asked by the media if he could confirm his victory was 'natural'. 'One hundred per cent, one hundred per cent,' said the jubilant winner. 'I think it's normal that people ask questions in cycling, given its history, but I know the sport has changed. There's absolutely no way I would be able to get these results if it hadn't. I certainly

know the results I'm getting won't be stripped 20 or 30 years down the line. Rest assured, that is not going to happen. For me, it is a bit of a personal mission to show that the sport has changed.' On day one of the Tour, the cover of *Le Monde* was emblazoned with a headline-grabbing quote from Lance Armstrong – 'It's impossible to win the Tour clean.' A closer look at the context of this line showed the headline ignored the qualifying phrase 'in my day' from the disgraced American's utterance, but it set the tone for the following three weeks. Whoever was in yellow would be pushed and prodded on the issue. The spectre of the Armstrong era remained. People desperately wanted to be able to believe in whoever stood on the top step of the podium.

Unlike Froome, Richie Porte was free on that particular day to reflect on his second place without having to fulfil media duties and doping-control tests. He felt on top of the world. 'The number one goal for me in the Tour was to support Chris. He'd had an outstanding season up to then, winning everything bar the Trentino. For me, even though I'd supported Chris throughout, I'd still come second to him in the Critérium International and the Dauphiné, so I did have GC ambitions of my own. The dream would have been a one–two finish, like Brad and Chris last year. After Ax 3 Domaines, yes, I did let myself dream of the podium in Paris, but the next day turned into the reverse of the day before . . . It was a disaster day.'

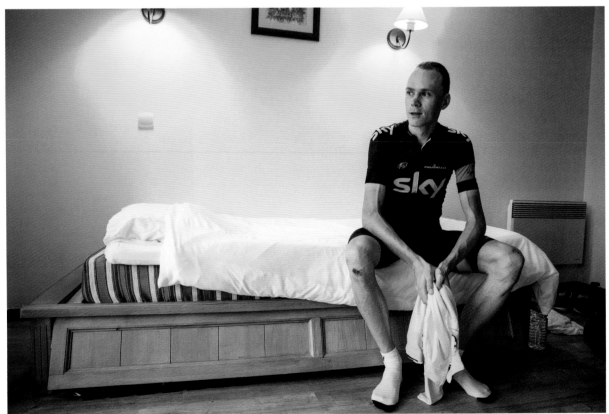

'The Sky train falls apart!' 'Off the rails!' 'Froomey isolated!' The headlines after the second day in the Pyrenees – and Team Sky's first outing to defend the yellow jersey – served half to report on the day's unbelievable action over four Category-1 climbs and half to alert all followers and competitors that the race was far from over. Just 29km after cresting the first climb, the Col de Portet-d'Aspet, Chris Froome found himself without any form of teammate buffer to protect him through wave after wave of attacks from the rivals and egos he had so humiliated and wounded with his dominant triumph on Ax 3 Domaines.

'They did go for me,' he nodded. 'It was tough being alone in front when the other teams had six or seven guys apiece, but I knew that no one on a physical level had the legs to beat me. Physically, I would be fine. I just had to play it right tactically. Nico, in the car behind me, was reminding me all the time that no one had been able to drop me the day before, so there was no reason why they would be able to today. Without Richie or Pete on the road with me, it was good to talk to someone. We looked at the major threats, maybe four or five guys, and decide that if any of them went, I would go too. Outside of that we would let the race run its course.'

'It was a hard day to manage,' said Portal. 'My job is to follow close behind Chris, but I was talking on the radio to everyone. To Froomey at the front – fine. Then to Richie – further back, unable to bridge, worried and upset. Then to Kiry at the back – I didn't need to give him any information or ideas. He was totally dead. My job is to keep up morale so I was telling Kiry he'd been doing a super-good job from the beginning to today . . . There'll be more races . . . It's just one race. Come on Kiry, *cou-rage*!'

It wasn't until Froome had made it safely to the line, retaining a lead of 1 minute and 25 seconds, declaring it was one of the hardest days he had ever experienced on a bike, that the full complexities of Team Sky's day were laid bare. The stage from Saint-Girons to Bagnères-de-Bigorre would go down as a day of multi-faceted drama all right. 'The stage started well, we were controlling it, though the pace was maybe too fast before the first mountain,' recalled Knaven. 'Then Peter crashed.'

Unfortunately nobody realised that Kennaugh, whose elbow had been clipped when he passed on the outside, had fallen down a steep ditch. 'There was nothing on Tour Radio so Nico passed the spot. Pete was five metres down! He was so angry. Just as I came round in the second car I saw him standing in the middle of the road. We quickly changed bike and helmet, and I was like "Pete crashed, Pete crashed" to Nico on the radio. It took

STAGE 9

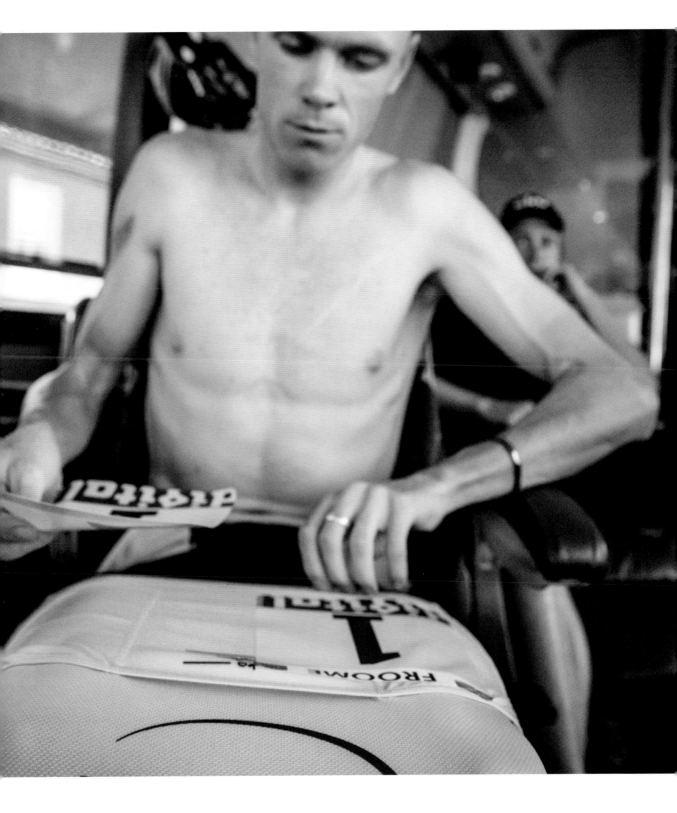

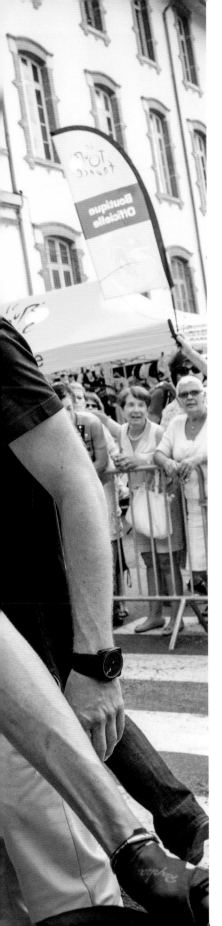

forever, riding full gas, before he was back in the peloton.' Physically, Kennaugh could count himself lucky: the impact broke his helmet. 'He was physically OK, with just cuts and bruises,' confirmed doctor Alan Farrell. 'But it was pretty shocking to see on TV. He literally fell off a cliff.'

The team, now strung out throughout the field, were out of their comfort zone. 'We were struggling to keep together,' said Boasson Hagen. 'I almost got Richie back on to help Chris, but then there would be another attack . . .' And so it went on. 'Richie had to help Chris by defending and chasing down every break,' said Portal. 'Richie tried to come back into the race, but he wasn't allowed by other teams because he was a threat in the GC. It then didn't make sense to expend energy. If you can't come back, you drop back and get to the finish in the time cut. That's why he backed off on the last mountain.'

'The thing is, we're probably the best-drilled team in the peloton, and we pride ourselves on being able to control things, but it was impossible to control the peloton that day,' recalled Porte. 'There was very little flat and then straight into a climb. It was just Chris and me and 40 guys who did not want me to be there. I couldn't fight that. It was a disaster. It could've been Tour Over had Chris not proved himself head and shoulders above the rest.'

While Porte plummeted from second to 33rd overall, Kiryienka had gone silent. No one knew how he was feeling. He didn't say anything to his team-mates. Ultimately, he missed the time cut. 'Kiry was unlucky. He had a bad day on a bad day to have a bad day,' said Cioni. 'Having to defend the leader's jersey against so many attacks, Kiry went really early that day and this caused his problem.'

For Froome, it was a case of 'all's well that ends well'. 'We felt positive in that we managed to keep the jersey on a bad day,' said Boasson Hagen. The way in which the team leader fended for himself, and remained unflappable, must have flummoxed his rivals. 'When we looked at the day in detail, we could see Chris responded perfectly blow by blow,' said Knaven. 'He was not too worried. It was just one day. He had a good cushion of time. He was always upbeat.'

While Portal admitted it was a satisfying stage for his own job fulfilment – 'Froomey needed me to be calm and for sure I lost one year of my life' – poor Kiryienka was forlorn. 'It was hectic at the end of that stage,' said Knaven. 'We had to catch a plane to Brittany and get to the hotel for dinner. Nico and I weren't on the same flight as the riders. As soon as we arrived we went to Kiry's room. He was really disappointed. We'd noticed in the Dauphiné that when it was very warm, he suffers. We felt the *grupetto* could have slowed down and helped him on the last mountain. His team-mates felt bad, especially Kosta, who was rooming with Kiry. He felt he could've helped him if he'd known he was suffering, getting him drinks or pushing him – and the team were disappointed because they were relying on him for the mountains.'

Vasili Kiryienka spent the rest day with the team, then flew home. His team-mates felt it was important to reaffirm team cohesion and authority on the road. Froome had emerged unscathed on the Bagnères-de-Bigorre stage – 'You could argue, using a boxing analogy, Chris has taken the biggest right hook on the chin he's going to take and he didn't flinch,' said Brailsford – but his survival was in part thanks to Movistar's decision to concentrate on distancing Porte, rather than attacking Team Sky's leader in numbers.

Geraint Thomas, double GB Olympic champion, drew on all his competitive resources to fuel the combative mood. 'The other teams see us as vulnerable and will try to take the race to us again,' he said. 'We see it as a fight now. It's like the track racing against the Aussies who we've always had a rivalry with. Coming up to London, we'd lost to them, but we turned it around when it mattered.'

'We had a long talk and everyone agreed we wanted to show that Team Sky was not falling apart,' said Boasson Hagen. 'We wanted to come back strong, work hard, each doing our own job 100 per cent to keep up the momentum for Chris.'

No details were divulged about evolving plans or strategies, but Brailsford was keen to emphasise there was positive energy to harness. 'We were dealing with more concentrated attacks this year than last,' he said. 'But when you have your backs to the wall it creates a bit of a

STAGE 10

siege mentality – and that's not a bad thing. It builds real camaraderie and self-belief.'

Richie Porte, for one, felt that Movistar had tried to get his place, and he wanted revenge. 'Losing Kiry, and no longer having Richie as number two on the GC – because that was a card we always wanted to play – had made it very hard,' recalled Froome. 'But that rest day was a turning point for us. We had a long talk. We put everything on the table. Where are we at? What do we need to move forward? We'd lost Kiry – an absolute machine and a fundamental part of the team. We had G with a broken pelvis. We were apprehensive, but we didn't want other teams to recognise that. We were struggling with the thought of how we were going to control it for another 12 days. We decided we would race with what we have and show our fighting spirit. It was amazing for me to see how everyone lifted themselves and found another 10 per cent.'

The gentle route to Saint-Malo had sprint finish written all over it. Crosswinds were forecast, but it proved a straightforward passage, with David López doing notable early work, sharing turns on the front with the sprint teams, before Boasson Hagen and Stannard stewarded Froome safely across the line. Back in ticking-off-day mode, Froome said: 'My guys did a super job keeping me out of trouble. Ian was an absolute bear in those conditions. All day the guys were chipping away and doing what was needed without losing any time.'

STAGE 11

There's no hiding for a rider in an individual time trial. It's one man and his bike against the clock, watched by everyone else. It's a test of handling skills, pacing and power output allied to mental toughness, nervelessness and extreme self-discipline. As Brailsford said, 'It's called the Race of Truth because you're on your own. No one else is involved. It's a question of how much you can push and hurt yourself over a given time in a given event. These guys figure out that feeling bad is probably good.'

With the Tour arriving in northern France, ferry loads of British cycling fans had taken up position along the 33km course from Avranches in Lower Normandy around the picturesque bay to Mont-Saint-Michel to enjoy the game of 'spot the approaching dot'. They wouldn't get the classic sight of the peloton flying past in a blur, complete with breakaway group and chasing pack, but they would have the opportunity to urge on individual 'home' riders such as Stannard, Thomas, Kennaugh and Froome as they came past, at roughly two-minute intervals, having departed in reverse order of their position in the general classification.

It was a day of relief from attacks from Movistar, Saxo-Tinkoff, Belkin, Orica, Garmin and co, but there were other, different potential hazards for Froome. A mechanical issue, such as the puncture that stymied Bradley Wiggins in the Giro? Worsening weather? But Froome was confident. During the winter he had spent time with the team, checking equipment and assessing his trialling posture in the wind tunnel at Southampton University. 'That was something I've never done before. We only had limited time, but it was still interesting to see the aerodynamic effects of different positions on the bike.' The gangly 28-year-old might not look as stylish in time-trial mode as Wiggins or world time-trial champion Tony Martin, but he knows how to get himself in the zone, how to maximise a pedal stroke, how to push himself to the limit using his power readings. On a day when the wind was buffeting ever stronger as the hours ticked by, he proved decisive and not a little intimidating in his all-yellow skin-suit and black bubble aero helmet pelting through the beautiful surroundings.

'You don't take any of the pictures in. You just go into tunnel vision,' he said. 'To get myself psyched up, I find it really helpful to go and see the course; then I go through it in my mind several times, visualising how I'm going to ride the different sections. I was really looking forward to this time trial. Most of my GC rivals were climbers. Trialling was not their particular strength, so I felt I had a bit of an advantage. I woke up that morning thinking, "Here I can get a huge advantage on these guys."'

Tony Martin was the man to watch. As the 64th competitor to roll down the start ramp thanks to his GC ranking of 118th, the German Omega Pharma-Quick Step rider posted a time of 36 minutes 29 seconds, covering the course at an average speed of 54.271 km/h. No other

rider had got within a minute of his benchmark time when Froome, last to go, set off. At the 9.5km mark, he had eclipsed Martin's time by one second. At the 22km post, he had a lead of 2.42 seconds. It was stunning to watch. Other former time-trial winners at the Tour weren't anywhere close to the pace set by Martin and being matched by Froome: Alberto Contador, who'd won in Annecy in 2009, was behind by 2 minutes 15 seconds; Cadel Evans, who'd won in Albi in 2007, lagged by 2 minutes 30 seconds.

Ultimately, the day was a contest between two riders with different goals: Martin, who wanted to win the stage, and Froome, who wanted to win the Tour. Martin got his reward at Mont-Saint-Michel, claiming his second stage victory ahead of the yellow jersey holder, who was thrilled to finish just 12 seconds behind after encountering strong headwinds in the final 2km.

'I was struggling to turn my legs,' said Froome. 'I was just trying to get to the finish. I was giving it everything because I'm going to need every second I can get, the way everyone is riding. I went absolutely full out. I was not quite expecting to be so close to Tony Martin's time. It was a huge boost to my confidence and great to get a nice buffer.'

The joy of witnessing the emphatic way in which Froome had re-established a comfortable lead reverberated throughout his team. 'He lost the stage to Tony Martin but he gained a huge margin over all his rivals,' marvelled Dario Cioni. 'It was clear then that he was the best rider in the field.'

For Nicolas Portal, gingerly following in the team car, it was a 'super, super' display. 'I was thinking this is where Chris wins the Tour. For the first ten days everyone takes the risk of attacking and throwing everything at him, but he keeps showing he's dominant.'

The event was important, too, for Richie Porte who restored his self-belief by powering to fourth behind Martin, Froome and Thomas De Gendt of Belgium. Froome, again showing his caring side as leader, was quick to emphasise his mate's triumphant bounce-back: 'Richie showed today he's certainly not out of this race. I'd expect him to be there in the mountains when we go into the Alps.'

'On the day after the disaster day, everyone was a bit shell-shocked,' recalled Porte. 'Dave B came up to me on the bus and said, "If you want to go for a good time trial, just do it." So I did. I finished fourth, and it was nice to show that had I not had that bad day I could have been right up there on the GC. It was satisfying because I proved something to myself as well. It's hard sometimes to stop thinking about the "what ifs". After the Bagnères-de-Bigorre stage, I thought, "You just have to get on with it." At the end of the day, it's one bike race of many, many races. The sun came up the next day, didn't it?'

With Chris Froome's rivals scattered, and ten days to survive until Paris, it was back to business as usual as Team Sky set off on the 218km trek from Fougères to a sprint finish in Tours determined to defend the yellow jersey and a lead of 3 minutes and 25 seconds. It was race business as usual, too, for Edvald Boasson Hagen, the team's versatile all-rounder. He might be a quiet presence off the bike and on the bus, but the Norwegian had proved in his three full seasons at Sky that he can unleash feisty bursts of speed to win from bunch sprints, breakaways and in time trials. He had been on fine form, narrowly missing out on a win on Stage 5, and holding second place overall on Stages 6 and 7.

'A cross between the Superbowl and a Justin Bieber concert' is how one team insider describes the high-intensity mayhem that accompanies the Tour convoy around France. As Norway's golden boy, Boasson Hagen is followed by a huge, shrieking fan club with a full repertoire of drinking songs. Today, however, they were to be silenced as it was Boasson Hagen's turn to suffer ill luck, crashing first at a late feeding zone, and then more seriously in a mass pile-up, as those with sprint-finish ambitions had upped the pace after the 3km sign. 'I was coming into the sprint on the same tactics as every other sprint,' he recalled. 'A guy went down in front of me. There was no place to go. I went over him and landed straight on my shoulder. It was very painful, but I could see that my collarbone was not broken, so I didn't think anything else was broken. G, with his broken pelvis, pushed me over the line – which was a bit funny! I got back to the bus and I was in a lot of pain – but I thought I'd be racing the next day, no problem. The doctor sent me for an X-ray and then I started to feel waves of excruciating pain. The verdict was a fractured right scapula. I've never been in so much pain before. This was a new level of pain.'

It's all too easy to fall off a bike at speed; riders are accustomed to suffering upper limb injuries as that part of the body tends to break a fall. Shoulder, elbow and wrist injuries are common. Rare is the rider who doesn't immediately recognise a break of the collarbone or clavicle, the long bone along which the force of impact is transmitted through the body. Following Wiggins's broken collarbone in 2010 and Siutsou's broken leg in 2011, it would be Boasson Hagen's turn to watch Team Sky's Tour campaign on television at home. Not that he was for withdrawing. 'Edvald said to me, "I've had a bad crash, but I can still help." He's such a good person,' recalls Nicolas Portal.

'Edvald's fracture was quite stable. It was always a non-operative injury, just a matter of him resting and

STAGE 12

recovering,' confirms team doctor Alan Farrell. 'He was disappointed and wanted to carry on. He and Geraint, who room together, are really pleasant, nice guys, and both tough cookies!'

Having had to adapt to an injured road captain, Geraint Thomas, and lost a vital climber in Kiryienka, the loss of Boasson Hagen – who in many other teams might be a team leader – was a significant blow. The Norwegian was Team Sky's only ever-present Tour member. He had been selected for the 2010, 2011, 2012 and 2013 editions – and now he was gone. Froome was left with six men in support. Two were débutants; one was fighting on with a fractured pelvis. 'It was a big moment for the management team when we saw Edvald crash and it was obvious he had a broken arm or shoulder,' said Rod Ellingworth. 'That's cycling. You can be at the heights of the world one day, the bottom the next day. The team could be all over the place, but Chris was confident that he could keep control. My job was to be buoyant about it. Every day there are crashes. If the riders are stressed or moody, it's up to the staff to stay happy, make the right decisions and say, "Right, this is what we are going to do about this." With Edvald, we got him straight into a medical programme at the Olympic Centre in Lillehammer and straight back into a performance schedule. Our attitude is, "It's happened. What's the practical solution? Never be emotional."'

Froome was understandably shaken by the loss of the man who is versatile on any gradient and who shared support duties with him on Bradley Wiggins's successful Tour. 'I only saw Chris look a bit worried twice,' said Cioni. 'When Kiry failed to make the time limit, and we'd been counting on him for the mountains, and when we lost Edvald.' But while the press officers helped protect Boasson Hagen from intense media interest and allowed him to make a calm, safe, dignified exit – just as they had for Wiggins in the Giro – the team principal had already processed the emotion and started to think tactically about how a seven-man Team Sky would continue.

'It's a shame for Edvald and a setback for the team because he's a versatile rider of huge ability, but I'm confident the riders we have left will pull together and see the race through. It's not ideal, but it's not the end of the world, either. The number of rivals we're going to have to mark is becoming less and less. If you put a line through everybody who's over a quarter of an hour down in this race, there's not a lot of blokes left. So it's a question of being more strategic and more tactically flexible.

'Ian Stannard has been coming into his own. We've adopted a different style, rather than having the whole team on the front trying to ride. It's a bit more manoeuvrable with Ian, who moves so well in the bunch, able to be more flexible and look after Chris. In these sprint stages, we now find it better to let the sprint teams get on with it and let Ian protect Chris in the final kilometres – and he's done a bloody good job of it.'

STAGE 13

The reduced team closed back in again and hit the road. 'Teams are going to throw everything they've got at us. This isn't going to be an easy ride to Paris and every day we have in yellow is an absolute honour,' said Froome before a day that, on paper, looked like an easy meander across flatlands to Saint-Amand-Montrond. Barely a third of the way in, Omega Pharma-Quick Step moved to the front and went at a furious pace, splintering the peloton into three groups. 'The Quick Step guys tired because they'd been going full gas, then crosswinds struck and Saxo-Tinkoff attacked.'

With 32km to go, Saxo-Tinkoff – led by former Team Sky road captain Mick Rogers – surged to the front, determined to split the peloton and distance the yellow jersey. Froome was with Stannard, Kennaugh and Thomas in a group that was behind by 20 seconds. At 10km to the finish, they lagged by 45 seconds. The gains for the leaders grew all the way to the finish, with the yellow jersey ultimately losing 1 minute 9 seconds to Alberto Contador.

For neutral observers, it was a brilliant racing move initiated by Rogers, who was now marshalling Contador rather than Wiggins. 'Mick knows Sky well. He said to his team, "Let's try," and they tried hard and they tried well!' recalled Portal. 'It was too hard to control everyone. In the car, on the radio, Chris was saying, "Yes, I'm losing time, I can't come back." It was a tricky stage. The race seemed to go on and on.'

'We had valued Mick at Sky for his experience and that experience doesn't go away when you move to a new team,' said Dario Cioni. 'Sometimes you race for your team against guys who are your training partners or friends or on the same national teams. You try to do everything you can to beat them on the road, but afterwards you're friends again. That day Mick did his job 100 per cent for another team.'

'I realised as soon as that attack went that it could be dangerous and I was in the wrong position because of the crosswinds,' explains Froome. 'I just switched off and thought I'm going to lose time, but knowing it was a big mountain day the next day I didn't want to kill myself chasing on the flat and in the wind. I would take a loss for what it was. I was grateful that I just lost a bit of time and didn't have my race ruined, like Alejandro Valverde, who punctured, couldn't get back because of the crosswinds and lost almost 10 minutes.'

That night, Team Sky and Saxo-Tinkoff stayed in the same hotel, one party jubilant, the other more subdued. 'It was a much better day for them than for us,' said Cioni. 'Dining that night in the same hotel, we were quiet, but we still had the jersey. We hadn't panicked because we had a cushion of time. We'd lost the battle but not the war!'

The Team Sky approach to achieving success in a Grand Tour is to focus not on the potential outcome but on the process needed to achieve the desired outcome on a day-by-day, if not hour-by-hour basis. 'I find taking that approach a very useful mentality,' says Froome. 'I aim to maximise time or reduce my losses each day. The Tour isn't a one-day race. You can't go flat-out. I concentrate on my aims day by day, but I do also need to be aware of what's coming up next.' Breaking the race down into concentrated sections is also a way to cope with the intensity of living in a high-pressure environment, 24/7, for three weeks, in close proximity to a small group while performing on one of the biggest platforms in world sport. Two weeks in, Peter Kennaugh expressed his gratitude to Nicolas Portal for his eve-of-race advice to take care to look after himself amid the mayhem. 'Pete said to me, "You're right. It's so different. Every ten seconds people try to jump in your face."'

Kennaugh was proving himself to be a strong rider, a big constant on the climbs and flat stages. As for Team Sky's other young warriors, Ian Stannard had come into the event declaring he had two roles: 'to work hard and then work even harder'. And he was duly hurting other teams by drilling it hard on the flat, keeping the breakaways in check, protecting Froome. Geraint Thomas was beginning to feel more comfortable. 'Every day I could sense that I was improving, growing stronger in my legs, and that gave me impetus. It was a question of being inspired by my team-mates, by what Froomey was doing in yellow. I wanted to do it for them. Edvald broke his shoulder blade in a fall and had to withdraw, but I realised I was fortunate in that I was injured in such a way as I could contribute.'

There is much tactical talk about protecting Froome, but the work of the staff behind the scenes is about diligent protection of all the riders on many levels. Both the Giro and the Tour highlighted the private roles of team doctors Richard Freeman and Alan Farrell, the care they dispense and the big decisions they have to make. The carers, led by the effervescent Mario Pafundi, take pride in providing the highest standards of comfort and hygiene to boost the riders' nightly recovery, as well as overseeing pre-race warm-up and post-race massages, and supplying them with *musettes*, energy gels and rehydrating drinks at feed zones and the finish line. The press officers anticipate what story will be the focus of intense interest and work to protect the dignity of the riders, while fulfilling media needs. The bus provides a haven. It was vital these strands wove together to keep the riders fresh and focused, for tomorrow it was Mont Ventoux . . .

STAGE 14

STAGE 15

The second weekend. Bastille Day. The 100th Tour de
France. On Sunday 14 July 2013, Mont Ventoux, aka the
'Beast of Provence' or 'God's Tomb', stood not just as a
geographical obstacle or an intimidating psychological
barrier wreathed in its spookily mythical aura; it was
also 'alive' with the tens of thousands of cycling fans
swarming in carnival mood along the roadside up to the
top. 'Riding through people who want to get so close to
you can be frustrating,' says Richie Porte of these tunnels
of claustrophobia. 'The vast majority do get out of the
way. Some are more interested in the TV camera than
in reaching out to the riders. To be honest, when you're
shepherding the yellow jersey, you don't take much in!'

The Ventoux needs no introduction to cycling
aficionados, but even those familiar with the tragic story
of Tom Simpson's death near its summit get a shiver
down their spine each time they experience the physical
transition of the climb from the Rhône valley floodplains
through coniferous forest and up to the surreal landscape
of barren bleached limestone where there's no escape from
a beating sun. The mountain marked the end of the longest
stage of the race: a *hors catégorie* ascent of just under
21km with a gradient that varied from 7.5 per cent to 12

per cent. While the early stages could prove quite tactical, Froome was confident that once he hit the mountain it was a straightforward matter of who had the legs. 'Today was always earmarked for us as a day where we could gain time,' he said. 'It becomes a case of who can dig deepest, who can suffer more.'

'It was a national holiday, Bastille Day, and the French were pretty motivated for it,' recalls Porte. 'Pierre Rolland attacked when Chris stopped, which you don't do . . . Europcar came up and rode absolutely superbly . . . It wasn't hard for us. They did our job for us until the last climb. Everyone was questioning how strong our team were with two men out and Geraint injured. First Europcar pulled, then Movistar took over, and then we took it up and smashed the descent, so we were in a great

position to start going up Mont Ventoux. Kosta was there, and Pete Kennaugh, who finished his turn with 9.5km to go. I led Chris for the next 2km, and that's when you see how strong our team were. He accelerated and the next bunch of favourites behind me took 5km to catch me! That was the key stage of the Tour. Froomey absolutely smashed it.'

As Froome recollects, once Porte peeled off, he put in two surges to bury Contador and race alongside the light little Colombian Nairo Quintana. 'Once Richie had finished his pull, I attacked Contador, got across and tried to get rid of Quintana,' he said. 'Two or three times, I passed him but he'd be straight back on to me. Still, he was five or six minutes behind me on the GC, so I wasn't worried. At 6 or 7km to go, I said to myself, there's no

doubt he's going to sprint to the finish and take the stage. I'd rationalised the idea of coming second. At 1.5km to go – and this was the biggest turning point – I saw Quintana had lost his legs. That was the split second when I realised I was going to win that stage.'

Froome accelerated ahead to win the stage by an astonishing 30 seconds, an effort that meant he needed oxygen at the top. The verdict on the Tour's official website was emphatic: 'Anyone who doubted the strength of Chris Froome and his Sky team at the 100th Tour de France was reminded that although two men are no longer there as support, the Kenyan-born Brit is The Dominant rider of the 2013 race. With great support from Peter Kennaugh and Richie Porte on the final climb – and a dream lead to the epic encounter on Mont Ventoux in the final 20km of the longest stage of this year's Tour – the leader of the Sky team put on a display of climbing that will be talked about for a long time to come. This was racing at its finest with clever, well-timed – and phenomenally strong – accelerations eliminating all of his rivals from the equation.'

'It was my second stage win,' said Froome, 'another mountain-top victory, on a landmark that is special in cycling history. To win it in the yellow jersey made it truly special. There had been a lot of talk about the yellow jersey riding in a defensive role, so I enjoyed taking the race on, dropping Quintana like that, and extending my lead. The biggest reason I went for it was we had a rest day the next day. Another motivator was that I knew I had my fiancée Michelle waiting for me at the top.'

Froome had pedalled clear at the memorial to Simpson, who in 1962 became the first Briton to wear the *maillot jaune*. 'It was just coincidence, but definitely worth paying tribute to him,' said Froome. 'Every cyclist would dream of winning a stage like today's. Just knowing the history of this climb, the guys who have won here before me, it's a really special feeling.'

Just as after Ax 3 Domaines, Froome's rivals conceded his brilliance. Alberto Contador led the comments: 'I don't think anyone can beat Froome uphill unless he has a bad day. I had enough trouble climbing at the pace I was, so *chapeau* to him.'

Emotions of pride, relief, joy, passion and competitive satisfaction were laced with defensive sarcasm as the team principal addressed the media. 'It's surprising, really, because the team isn't good enough. You think we have had a difficult couple of days and you think we have got a shit team, but we think we're doing all right,' Brailsford said. 'People have been questioning the team all week. We have had a few challenges but you never write off a good team. When we are pushed, prodded and challenged, and sometimes unfairly criticised, like the stick Chris has taken, sometimes the best way to reply is with your legs. And that's what Chris has done. It's quite emotional. The 100th Tour, Bastille Day, one of the iconic stages, and this mountain with its particular emotional attachment for British cycling with Tommy Simpson. For a team who have taken quite a bit of stick, the best way to bounce back is a performance like that.'

Ask team members to nominate a high and a low from the Tour, and many give one answer: Mont Ventoux. On the one hand, Froome's superlative performance was breathtaking; on the other, it prompted questions, not about sporting prowess, but about whether it was 'clean'. The spectre created by Lance Armstrong's revelations just would not go away.

Dave Brailsford sat side by side with his rider at the rest-day press conference. 'We have a great performance and I jump for joy, and ten minutes later I guarantee I will be answering these allegations and questions about doping for the next few days,' he had said. 'Chris has remained strong and calm and very confident. He has never flinched. He doesn't make Churchillian speeches, but he has demonstrated in adversity and extreme conditions – and with all the questioning – that he can handle himself in a robust and calm manner, which is very rare. He has stayed polite, calm, rational. You can't fault him.'

It was true. 'It's quite sad that the day after the biggest victory of my life, we're talking about doping,' Froome said, with restraint yet strength of feeling. 'We've slept on volcanoes, been away from home for months, working our asses off to get ready for this, and here I am, basically being accused of being a cheat and a liar – that's not cool.

'I can only be open and say I've trained extremely hard to get here. All the results I get are the product of determination. It's really been a long battle to get to where I am. I've got the support of a fantastic team and to talk of anything outside of that, I can't. I don't know about any of that stuff. I know what I've done to get here and I'm extremely proud of it. I can understand why people are asking, given the history of the sport – they've been let down so many times before. But I'm also one of those people who's been let down. I've also believed in people who've turned out to be cheats and liars. But I can assure you, I'm not.'

Typically open, and wanting to solve a problem, Brailsford invited the inquisitors to help. 'You tell me, what could we do so we wouldn't have to answer the same question over and over?' Following up on the buzz-phrase 'power data', he suggested the team could share their power data information with the World Anti-Doping Agency, but not the public, thus protecting the team's professional advantages but also making them subject to scrutiny. 'They can have everything we've got. They can come and live with us. They can come and dig up all our information. They can see all our data, have access to every single training file we've got and then they can compare the training files to the blood data to weight. WADA would be a body with the right expertise to analyse that data. And then

STAGE 16

they can tell the world whether it's credible or not.'

Six weeks later, Brailsford put that day into context. 'The media feeding frenzy gets into full swing at the Tour de France. You face the media the moment you get off the bus in the morning and then straight after the day's race. That's twice a day for 21 days. I found the media interesting to watch as a group. Certain stories ebb and flow. Certain aspects catch on, for example the phrase "power data". Nobody was talking about power data before the Tour de France. It wasn't on the agenda, but it became *the* talking point. It was the first Tour de France after the Lance Armstrong revelations, so it was all about the level of trust. It's a very strange situation. The sport is cleaner now than ever but because of the revelations of past riders, the sport is getting closer scrutiny and riders are having to take this because of the misdemeanours of the past. I think a lot of the media were wondering, did we ask enough questions before? They were questioning each other about the level of questioning in the Armstrong era; there had always been rumours and talk, but did they follow it up? There was a general feeling that they needed to ask tough questions – and we were on the receiving end of that. Reporters have a duty to ask the questions, but they also set the tone. Riders are smart enough to understand why they were being asked, but it still doesn't make it easy. '

Froome, too, gave his perspective. 'Since I'd been in the yellow jersey, those had been the questions. I thought

EDMONDSON
EISEL
FROOME
HAYMAN
HENAO
KENNAUGH
KIRYIENKA
KNEES
LOPEZ
PATE
PORTE
PUCCIO
RASCH
ROWE
SIUTSOU
STANNARD
SUTTON
SWIFT
THOMAS
TIERNAN - LOCKE
URÁN
WIGGINS
ZANDIO

that, a week on, those questions would subside, but my performance on Ventoux added to the scepticism and doubts,' he said. 'I do get that people have been left in doubt in the past, but it does get frustrating. My form was not something that has come out of the blue. It was the result of a lot of calculated preparation. It does add up, and I was getting frustrated at pointing that out, time and time again. It was getting irritating when the racing itself was so exciting. It was a great shame for the Tour.'

As Froome's regular room-mate, Richie Porte was exposed to his mood: 'I know Chris Froome. We train together, we room together. His performance is due to nothing more than the fact that he is physiologically the best and he trains the best. We knew anyone who was in the yellow jersey would get the questions, but people need to go back and ask why the guys who used to beat Chris now can't . . .'

Six days to go; there was still tough racing to survive. The Portuguese Rui Costa took the win on Stage 16, and Froome survived a nasty moment when Contador, attacking on the last descent, overcooked a corner, putting him at risk. 'He was pushing the limits around the corners when he crashed in front of me,' said Froome. 'I had to go off the road to get around him. I don't think it was necessary to take those kinds of risks. There's no such thing as an uneventful day here. If they're not attacking on the climbs, they're attacking on the descents.'

STAGE 17

Imagine the thoughts of Chris Froome's rivals as they prepared to counter him in another individual time trial. The Briton had taken a chunk of time in the previous test to Mont Saint-Michel; he had subsequently gained time with emphatic mountain-top finishes at Ax 3 Domaines and Mont Ventoux. And here he was again, preparing to take them on over an uphill 32km course from Embrun to Chorges.

But the momentum of a race can alter swiftly. Had Froome's criticism of Contador's dangerous descending into Gap ignited new determination in the Spaniard? Would tomorrow's impending challenge of the double ascent of the Alpe d'Huez make it difficult to gauge effort today? Did the first downpour of rain signify a threat? Would the mooted switch from Dogma road bike to time-trial Bolide at the 20km mark upset rhythm? These questions were all answered with a steadfast 'no' thanks to another brilliant piece of forensic planning by Team Sky and Chris Froome to maintain superiority on the road.

After a morning reconnaissance, the team decided a switch of bike models could make a crucial difference, using bigger gears on the straightish, flattish run down to the finish. This would require a pre-planned 'pitstop' and a speedy manoeuvre from mechanic Gary Blem and *DS* Nicolas Portal. Most riders opted to use standard road bikes for the entire course. Setting off last on a drying road surface, Froome paced himself beautifully to secure his first victory in a time trial at the Tour de France, his third stage win in 2013 and the fourth of his career. He crossed the line, beating Contador by 8.82 seconds – even though the Spaniard had not interrupted his ride to swap bikes – stretching his advantage over the second-placed Saxo-Tinkoff man to a full 4 minutes and 34 seconds.

'I can't believe I won,' he mused afterwards. 'I wasn't going to empty myself. I expected to lose 30 seconds to a minute today. I went into today thinking I was going to try and limit my losses, thinking about the days to come. To go through the finish line with the fastest time – I didn't see that coming. The bike change could very well have been the difference. When I rode the route this morning I felt I needed the bigger gearing for the last descent. The run-in was really fast so I made sure I had bigger gears on that second bike to be able to push on coming into the final.'

The big loser was Bauke Mollema, who had been in second place overall, but ended up 6 minutes and 23 seconds behind Froome in the GC.

Four days to go, but three were monstrous Alpine stages. Tomorrow's double ascent of the Alpe d'Huez would introduce a level of insanity beyond the physical challenge. According to the writer Tim Moore, the mountain 'annoys the purists but enthrals the broader public, like 20/20 cricket or beach volleyball . . . When the Tour goes up Alpe d'Huez, it's a squalid, manic and sometimes lethal shambles . . . like the Glastonbury Festival for cycling fans.'

'L'Alpe d'Huez was my worst day of the Tour,' recalled Nicolas Portal. 'I was alone at the front, following Chris, when I had a problem with my car. It turned out there was too much ice in the cool box for drinks. Some of the ice melted and a lot of water escaped and went all over the electrics. Everything in the car stopped. I didn't have a battery. I was on the mountain in the middle of extraordinary crowds. I couldn't take care of the riders and I couldn't contact them. It was quite stressful! And worse, I was worried it was dangerous. I was imagining calling to say, "I'm on fire!"'

Long before Portal encountered his mechanical problem, the action had settled into a reassuring rhythm. A nine-man break was allowed up the road as Team Sky, driven by Thomas and Stannard, settled into a tempo en route to the first passage over the famous Alpe. Kanstantsin Siutsou and David López took over to pace the lead group up the climb through a wall of fans, some of whom were drunk, scary and abusive. On the devilish descent that the riders had feared, Contador and team-mate Roman Kreuziger made their move. 'We came up to the top of Alpe d'Huez for the first pass, then got through the descent, where Contador attacked as expected,' recalls Richie Porte. 'It was when we were going through the valleys I realised we had a problem. Pete Kennaugh went to get *bidons*, but he couldn't get any bottles of drink because the car wasn't there. Apparently there'd been a leak which had circuited the car.'

STAGE 18

After great work from Kennaugh, Movistar finally arrived at the front to shut things down before the final ascent of the epic climb. 'We started the last ascent, and had 10 or 11km to go when I saw Chris have a hunger attack. I thought, "Shit, he's got good legs today, but he's fighting hunger." We weren't able to feed before the climb because of the problems with the car. There are eating rules which state that no rider can collect food from the team car within the last 6km, so we decided I should go all the way back to the car and get an energy gel. They usually cost a couple of Euros but this one ended up being quite expensive, costing in total about 2,000 Euros! Chris and I both took a time penalty and a fine penalty. Nico also took a fine. But I understand: rules are rules.'

'I can assure you that's not the first time in my career I've run out of sugar,' said Froome. 'I'm just happy to get out of the stage with my lead increased, so if that was a bad day for me, I'll definitely accept that. I was having a tough time. This was definitely the hardest day, but I think that's to be expected. Two times up Alpe d'Huez and this late in the race, it's definitely a hard day, especially keeping in mind what's coming up tomorrow.'

Froome was quick to praise his wingman's emergency sustenance run. 'Richie Porte is a really great guy. I mean, he put aside all his ambitions in this race to help keep the jersey on my shoulders and he did such a good job today – really fantastic. He paced me through that whole climb

basically. It was really hard to talk on that climb, there was just so much noise going through all those people. To be able to talk, we had to get really close to each other, but it was just talking to dictate what pace we should carry on at just to try and get through the stage. It was a really hard day but I think, all in all, it's a really good day for us – just extending the lead on general classification [to 5 minutes 11 seconds over Contador]. Also, something else about today: it's Nelson Mandela Day and I would like, from my point of view, to inspire a lot of young Africans to be able to achieve their ambitions.'

On another positive note came the announcement that independent sports scientist Fred Grappe had concluded from the in-house details of 18 of Froome's climbs since his breakthrough in the 2011 Vuelta – handed over to *L'Equipe* by Dave Brailsford following the Mont Ventoux press conference – that the results were consistent with doping-free cycling. 'I'm really happy to hear these findings, to hear their take on it, because it's basically backing us up to say these performances are very good, strong, clean sporting performances,' said Froome. 'It's good that someone's actually been allowed to see the data and after seeing it, has come back and said, "Actually these guys are doing it right, they seem to be doing things according to what we'd expect."'

STAGE 19

After the double demands of the Alpe d'Huez it seemed incredible that the field were required to embark on a 204.5km chase through the Alps over five categorised climbs. Team Sky set off braced for the onslaught of last-ditch assaults on the yellow jersey. A breakaway disappeared up the road as Thomas, Stannard and the rest set about pacing the peloton over some of the toughest climbs of the race, but, in the course of the six-hour trek from Bourg-d'Oisans to Le Grand-Bornand, sustained attacks from Froome's rivals never materialised.

'I'm at a bit of a loss to explain it,' mused Brailsford. 'Chris and Richie didn't have to work. Today was all or nothing if someone wanted to risk it.' No one did, at least not with real intent, although Contador, Quintana and Joaquim Rodríguez had one lacklustre burst over the last section of the final climb. Froome, faithfully shepherded as ever by Richie Porte, came down off the fast descent of the Col de la Croix Fry in the rain to finish as part of an elite group who were all awarded the same time at the finish, with Froome maintaining that satisfying cushion of a 5 minute 11 second lead over Alberto Contador.

'There was definitely a sigh of relief after today's stage,' said Froome. 'This was one of the stages I was most worried about. On paper it was the one with the most climbing on it. With the weather the way it was, too, there was a lot of potential for things to get out of hand. I was ready for anything, especially after the way the Tour has gone so far. The guys did take it up and attack on that final climb, and they did go pretty quickly down the other side of it in the rain, but I'm glad that stage is behind us. I'm just thankful for my team-mates for getting me this far today – they did a huge job.'

'Nineteen days into a Grand Tour and everyone was feeling it,' recalled Froome later. 'I had a lead of five minutes plus so everyone had given up the fight a bit mentally. The agenda had changed. Some teams were just desperate to get something out of the race, for example Saxo-Tinkoff going for the team prize position.'

While the outside world was depicting Froome as a champion in waiting, as a hero on the brink of immortality, Brailsford insisted his team would roll out tomorrow 'with the fear of God in us to defend what we have'. There was no room yet for relief or complacency. The 'fine line' is the basis of the Team Sky philosophy: the line between losing and winning, between failure and success, between good and great, between dreaming and believing, between convention and innovation, between heart and head. There would be no let-up until Paris for the mechanics working until 1am to clean and prepare the bikes for the next day, for Søren in the kitchen trying to stimulate fatigued riders with enticing food, for the Jaguar team car mechanics and bus driver, for the carers who did everything from preparing the riders' anallergic bedding and thermogel mattresses to doing a daily 10kg kit wash, from preparing *bidons* and *musettes* to ensuring the riders each received at least an hour's massage treatment every evening.

'We are the "marginal gains" team,' says lead carer Mario Pafundi. 'The full complement of staff behind the scenes are not on the camera, but we do every job 110 per cent. Dave Brailsford said to me, "Mario, everyone in the team's playing an instrument and we have to make sure everyone plays their part well because, if they don't, it won't make a good sound."' For the carers, a Grand Tour lasts far longer than 21 days of racing and two rest days. A week before, they travel out to the team service course in Mechelen, Belgium, to pack equipment: *bidons*, helmets, rain packs, energy products, bedding and food items. During the race, they multi-task at the hotel, feed zones, finish line and on the bus. They have to be as proficient at applying kinesiology tape as at vacuuming hotel rooms, at setting up the mobile laundrette and sorting out the hotel rooms, at remembering who has requested the mango rehydration drink and who gets the gluten-free *musettes*.

Sky have five carers for nine riders. 'Each carer looks after two riders, but the person with one rider does not have the best job. He has to have all the equipment washed clean and ready for the next day!' jokes Pafundi. Laundering for the team requires six daily washes at high temperatures (for extra hygiene) and drying sessions. 'The riders have spare kit, but this year Chris Froome liked the fit of his first yellow jersey, so he wanted the same one all the way through – even though the organisers gave him a new one each day. He was a bit superstitious. We had to wash it every night for him.'

Since arriving in the Alps, Chris Froome had gone to bed thinking, 'OK, I've got this five-minute advantage, but at any second something's going to challenge that. I've been so fortunate so far, not to have a mechanical at the wrong time. A crash. Anything going wrong.' Realistically, the near round trip today from Annecy to Annecy-Semnoz was the last day he had to survive those fears while combating steep gradients. The competitive focus at the 2013 Tour de France had become all about the race for second place. Contador had only 21 seconds of advantage over the flying climber, Nairo Quintana, while the Spaniard Joaquim Rodríguez had ridden into feisty form.

It's not Froome's style to sit back. On the final summit finish – the yellow jersey safe on his back – he joined the fray with those dicing for second place, unleashing a trademark burst of acceleration on the climb to bridge across to Rodríguez and Quintana. The Colombian kicked on to claim the stage win – pulling himself up to second on the Paris podium in the process. Rodríguez hung on for second, elevating himself to third. For the commentators, the day was all about 'Christopherrrr Frooooome', who concluded his general classification campaign in style. Again, his performance was backed up by an impressive effort from his team-mates. Team Sky had hit the bottom of the 10.7km final ascent hard with Stannard and Thomas stringing it out, then Siutsou, López and Kennaugh taking it up to thin out the lead group. Richie Porte finished the stage fifth, to round off a strong day for the team. All the magnificent seven had to do was ride safely on to the Champs-Elysées to secure back-to-back Tour victories for Great Britain and Team Sky.

'It's hard waking up on the penultimate day and not wishing it's already over, especially when it's such a hard stage,' said Porte. 'But the race went well. The job was done. And then you get this incredible sense of relief when you get back to the bus. We allowed ourselves one beer!'

Froome – going round the post-race triangle of podium, press and doping control – was a mix of modesty, pride and relief personified. 'I can't quite believe I'm sitting here in this position. This really is amazing. I'm a bit lost for words,' he managed to say. 'We still have to roll into Paris tomorrow but this is it, this is the GC side of it pretty much sorted out, and to finish it off like this is really special. It was quite hard to stay on top of it once I got to about 3km to go. That's where it sunk in that this is it: I've accomplished what I needed to . . . I was just following the wheels, just overwhelmed by the feeling of, "OK, this is it now, I'm safe and I've got pretty much to the finish."'

Back at the hotel there were glasses of champagne,

and a feast of burgers and pizzas from Søren. 'I always find it strange to start celebrating the day before,' mused Froome. 'It doesn't rest easy with me. But, given the last stage is traditionally a procession on to the Champs-Elysées – and I don't think anyone's ever lost a yellow jersey on the final day – I guess we're safely there.'

For the press officers, who daily absorb the

STAGE 20

overview of the Team Sky bubble within the bigger scheme of things, the victory was extra special. 'The Tour is an extraordinary race because of the tensions that inevitably arise,' said Dario Cioni. 'It's not a regular challenge, so the happiness when you finish, and finish with a victory, is incredible. You set out with goals, you meet them despite all the uncontrollables, and the satisfaction is even greater. The Tour is hard work for every team member, full of the unexpected events that you have to manage in the best possible way. For all the support staff, at the training camps and other races too, Chris's victory was a big, big reward. For the team to win the Tour de France for the second consecutive year was unbelievably special.'

The temperature was scorching in Paris. Mobile phones and tablets went into meltdown. Crowd-control barriers sunk into molten Tarmac. Spectators fanned themselves as they sat, securing their position, on chairs that folded out from the commemorative backpacks available from the official Tour de France mobile boutiques (and sold out within hours). *L'Equipe* ran with the headline *Le Roi Soleil* in anticipation of the moment the absolute ruler of the GC contenders would arrive on the famous cobbles to be crowned the champion of the 2013 Tour de France. A night-time finish had been scheduled for the 100th edition of the Tour. The Arc de Triomphe was lit up in yellow. The length and breadth of the entire Champs-Elysées was packed with fans of many nationalities decked out in yellow hats, umbrellas and T-shirts. All places had been taken up by 2pm, a full six hours before the riders were due to hit the chestnut-lined avenue.

At 5.45pm, Chris Froome, resplendent in the yellow jersey for the 13th consecutive day, rolled out of Versailles on an all-yellow bike, wearing yellow helmet, yellow framed sunglasses and black-and-yellow commemorative shoes ('which were pretty uncomfortable,' he confided, 'but it was for only just over 100 kilometres'). The170-strong peloton had ridden around the gardens of the Palace of Versailles before the traditional festivities started with champagne-sipping and photo-taking amongst the riders. Froome even had a puff on a fat cigar.

'That moment signified "Job done, Tour won,"' said an emotional Nicolas Portal with satisfying simplicity.

The Sky team led the peloton on to the Champs-Elysées for the first of ten laps, culminating in a last-burst sprint to the line, with Froome giving his 'absolute gem' of a team-mate, Richie Porte, the honour of leading the bunch for the first lap. 'Traditionally, the yellow jersey team leads everyone on to the Champs-Elysées,' said the Australian. 'As we approached, Chris came up beside me and said, "You're going to lead us on to the Champs-Elysées." I'm not an emotional person, but when he said that my hair was standing on end. It's the nicest gesture anyone has ever made to me.'

Team Sky did the whole first lap at the front of the bunch, then left the sprint teams to begin their lead-outs and jostling. In the final acceleration – where at 9.32pm Marcel Kittel edged out André Greipel and Mark Cavendish, denying the Manxman what would have been a record fifth consecutive win in the final stage of the Tour – Froome and his valiant six team-mates dropped well behind. A minute later, illuminated only by the headlamps of the cars following behind, Team Sky's leader would

STAGE 21

cross the line arm-in-arm with David López and Richie Porte, who in turn had linked arms with Ian Stannard, Geraint Thomas, Peter Kennaugh and Kanstantsin Siutsou.

'I got the feeling that people weren't taking in what a team effort racing in the Tour is, so I thought it would be nice to make a gesture that emphasised the fact I couldn't have won it alone,' said Froome. 'It went down well. I think it was nice for my team-mates to share that experience. Having taken the yellow jersey on Stage 8, there'd been a lot of defending to do.'

Just as it had promised on the eve of their campaign back in Corsica, the Tour had put each member of Team Sky through an exacting and enriching experience. 'This year, with a younger team, when we'd lost a few guys and with G coming through with injury, it felt like the most deserved victory,' agreed Porte. 'It was Chris's idea to have our own celebration as we crossed the line. The plan was to stick at the back and come across together with linked arms. That was something I'll never forget for the rest of my life.'

For Rod Ellingworth, the sight of Peter Kennaugh

riding into Paris summed up the venture. 'This guy was on his knees, but when he rolled past the Eiffel Tower, you could see he was a young lad and what it meant to him. The way the lads crossed the line, deliberately dropping back and linking arms – I wasn't sure they should do that – but it was very much driven by Chris as a generous gesture of thanks to his team-mates.'

So Christopher Froome – as the French persisted in calling him, despite his bemusement ('Honestly, I don't really like my full name') – became the winner of the 100th Tour de France with an advantage of 4 minutes 20 seconds. He became the second British champion of the Tour, the first rider born in Africa to take home the *maillot jaune* and a symbol of a bright future for the Tour. The youth of the three men who garnered the jerseys was notable – Froome, 28, Nairo Quintana (young rider and mountain) and Peter Sagan (points) both 23; three young talents entering their prime.

'We saw a new side to Chris,' said Cioni. 'But it wasn't his metamorphosis into a team leader. We'd seen his leadership ability in the build-up races all year. The biggest

change was when he went from wearing the yellow jersey to being a champion. He won the 100th edition and he won four individual stages, including Mont Ventoux. It was an incredible way to achieve champion status.'

As if in honour of his tally of four stage wins, Froome was called up on to the podium four times: to receive the sequinned yellow jersey for the brightest star of the centenary edition, to be honoured with the top three finishers in the general classification, to stand with the full complement of jersey winners, and finally to be included in the presentation of a sequined yellow jersey to Bernard Hinault, Eddy Merckx and Miguel Indurain. "That was special," he said. "They are icons of the sport, each with five plus Tour wins. It was surreal."

After dedicating his victory to his late mother, Jane, and reassuring the crowds that 'this is one yellow jersey that will stand the test of time', the 2013 Tour de France champion stepped down from the podium and paused to take stock: 'Crossing the line with the guys brought tears to my eyes. I expected it to be big, but all of this is something else.'

THE TOUR IN DETAIL

> 'Going into the Tour felt similar in many respects to last year, but instead of thinking it was our title to defend, which would have been a negative mindset, we went out to try and win it a second time starting from zero.'
>
> Sir Dave Brailsford

ROUTE / The 100th edition kicked off in Corsica with a rare road stage to decide the first recipient of the yellow jersey. The opening test traced the island's east coast, heading out of Porto-Vecchio, looping south to Bonifacio and the Category-4 Côte de Sotta, before continuing north on undulating coastal roads. The flat finale promised an all-out drag race to the line.

HOW IT UNFOLDED / Drama at both the start and the finish. Chris Froome's campaign began with a jolt as he hit a kerb and went down in the neutralised zone before rejoining with a new bike ahead of the flag drop.

A five-man breakaway powered away to fight for the first polka dot jersey (won by Juan José Lobato). Anticipating a hectic sprint finish, the peloton kept close tabs on the breakaway in a disjointed chase. With 35km to go, Team Sky hit the front to regain control.

In a bizarre scenario, the Orica-GreenEDGE team bus became wedged under an overhead gantry, blocking the finish line. A new finish was mooted, then switched back as the bus was dislodged. Cue carnage. Ian Stannard and Geraint Thomas crashed, as did Peter Sagan and Alberto Contador; pre-stage favourite Mark Cavendish was also held up. Chaos ensured a reduced bunch headed into Bastia, with Marcel Kittel claiming the first yellow jersey. Then it was announced that because of the confusion all riders would be given the same time.

STAGE 1 RESULT:

Winner. Marcel Kittel (Ger); Argos-Shimano; 04h 56' 52"
2. Alexander Kristoff (Nor); Katusha; @ same time
3. Danny van Poppel (Ned); Vacansoleil-DCM; @ same time

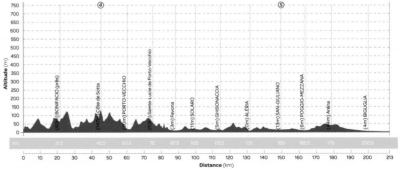

Stage 1
CHAOS IN CORSICA
Saturday 29 June / Porto-Vecchio to Bastia, 213km

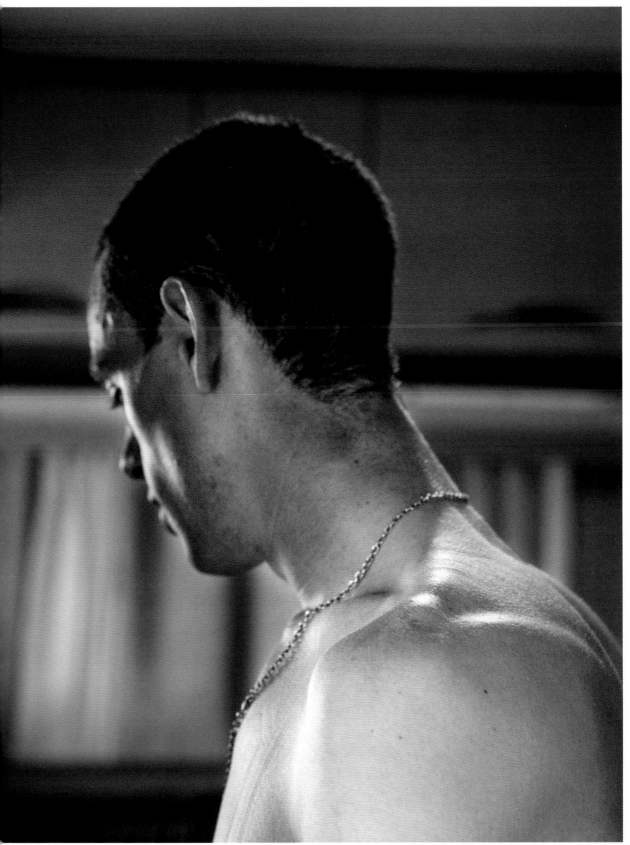

ROUTE / The Tour's middle day on Corsica wound south-west towards the capital of Ajaccio across the mountainous spine of the island, producing an intriguing cross-country stage featuring four categorised climbs and a 12km flat finish.

HOW IT UNFOLDED / Avoiding trouble was the priority after the crash-strewn and controversial opening stage, but drama returned when a dog wandered across the road in front of the peloton just as six riders were establishing a lead inside the final 5km.

Unfazed, Tour débutant Jan Bakelants went for glory with one kilometre remaining and held on for the victory. He celebrated the first stage win of his professional career with the yellow jersey, while Peter Sagan led the peloton home 1 second behind.

Chris Froome came home in the peloton after riding clear of the bunch on the final climb of the day, 12km from the finish in Ajaccio. Having followed Richie Porte up the first 700m of the 1km climb, Froome took his rivals by surprise with a sharp burst of speed to ensure he could take the tricky descent at his own pace. Mission accomplished, he crossed the line 1 second behind Bakelants to move up to 18th overall.

Stage 2
THRILLING THE CROWDS
Sunday 30 June / Bastia to Ajaccio, 156km

STAGE 2 RESULT:
Winner. Jan Bakelants (Bel); RadioShack-Leopard; 03h 43' 11"
2. Peter Sagan (Svk); Cannondale; +00' 01"
3. Michal Kwiatkowski (Pol); Omega Pharma-Quick Step; +00' 01"

OVERALL STANDINGS:
1. Jan Bakelants (Bel); RadioShack-Leopard; 08h 40' 03"
2. David Millar (GB); Garmin-Sharp; +00' 01"
3. Julien Simon (Fra); Sojasun; +00' 01"

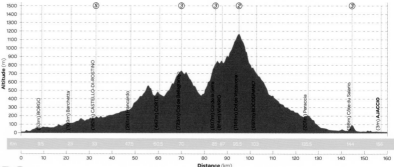

ROUTE / Another day of vigilance for GC contenders. A rollercoaster route headed north on mountainous coastal roads, hitting Category-4 Col de San Bastiano 12km in. A brief flat run introduced further climbing, intensifying at Col de San Martino, which marked the start of a relentless run to the finish over narrow, winding roads. An inviting straight descent on the run-in fuelled the prospect of a sprint finish.

HOW IT UNFOLDED / The toughest stage so far. A five-man breakaway pushed clear out of Ajaccio with RadioShack-Leopard, Belkin, Saxo-Tinkoff and Team Sky keen to take up the mantle and assert themselves on the climbs.

Team Sky hit the front on numerous occasions to establish position for Chris Froome, who finished the day safely in a reduced peloton alongside Edvald Boasson Hagen and Richie Porte.

Attacks fired off over the top of the Col de Marsolino but the peloton fended off the moves to set up a sprint, in which Simon Gerrans timed his burst of speed perfectly to inch out Peter Sagan. The bunch finish worked to the advantage of Jan Bakelants, who hung on to his lead after his team committed numbers to control the stage.

Geraint Thomas rode through the pain barrier in a valiant display to complete the stage. Secondary medical checks had revealed a small fracture in his pelvis following his Stage 1 crash.

STAGE 3 RESULT:
Winner. Simon Gerrans (Aus); Orica-GreenEDGE; 03h 41' 24"
2. Peter Sagan (Svk); Cannondale; @ same time
3. José Joaquín Rojas (Esp); Movistar; @ same time

OVERALL STANDINGS:
1. Jan Bakelants (Bel); RadioShack-Leopard; 12h 21' 27"
2. Julien Simon (Fra); Sojasun; +00' 01"
3. Simon Gerrans (Aus); Orica-GreenEDGE; +00' 01"

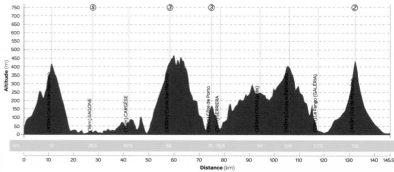

Stage 3
SPECTACULAR ANTICS
Monday 1 July / Ajaccio to Calvi, 145.5km

ROUTE/ An out-and-back course along the Mediterranean coast skirted around Parc Phoenix before heading north for a quick loop, taking in the intermediate split at 13km. A largely pan-flat course with limited technicality conjured up a test of pace and strength for each squad.

HOW IT UNFOLDED/ Team Sky powered in to the course to clock a time of 25' 59", enabling Chris Froome to put time into all his GC rivals.

Riding as a unit, the team crossed the line with eight of the nine riders together, Geraint Thomas again riding through pain to arrive moments later. The team finished 3 seconds back on Orica-GreenEDGE and two seconds behind Omega Pharma-Quick Step, who set the early benchmark. Alberto Contador's Saxo-Tinkoff squad were fourth quickest.

The result ensured Edvald Boasson Hagen, Froome and Richie Porte occupied sixth, seventh and eighth overall, 3 seconds behind new race leader Simon Gerrans.

'If we had taken yellow it would mean that tomorrow and the next couple of days, which are predominantly flat, we'd be on the front doing all that work, which I think would be a bit unnecessary at the moment for such a small advantage,' said Froome. 'It gives us a few more days to be in the peloton and we'll wait until the mountains come, where I feel the team will really excel.'

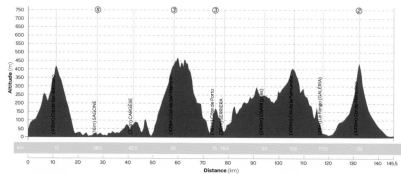

Stage 4
UNITED WE RIDE
Tuesday 2 July / Nice, 25km, Team Time Trial

ROUTE/ A tricky day in the medium mountains; a perfect day for a breakaway. The route rolled westward through the Provençal hills via four climbs that were categorised but not tough enough to put off the sprinters. A finely balanced stage open to committed riders of different types – sprinters, explosive climbers, breakaway artistes.

HOW IT UNFOLDED/ Six riders attacked early, building a lead that stretched to more than 12 minutes. Orica-GreenEDGE stepped up the chase in the last 70km, and the final rider was reeled back in the final 4km by a peloton flying with sprint teams trying to assert their authority at the front of the bunch. Omega Pharma-Quick Step proved the most effective, each rider peeling off in turn to launch Mark Cavendish.

Edvald Boasson Hagen came within a whisker of his third Tour stage win, but was edged into second place by Cavendish after a flat-out finish in Marseilles. The Norwegian did brilliantly to latch on to Cavendish's wheel, but couldn't round the Manxman, who seized his 24th Tour stage career win.

Peter Sagan took the remaining place on the podium, with all the main GC contenders present in a considerable front group, which ensured Boasson Hagen, Froome and Richie Porte defended their sixth, seventh and eighth places respectively in the overall standings.

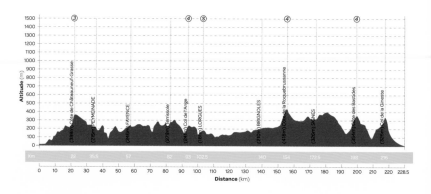

Stage 5
FLAT-OUT FINISH
Wednesday 3 July / Cagnes-sur-Mer to Marseilles, 228.5km

207

ROUTE / A second roll-out for the sprinters as the route dipped out of Aix before heading west. The dynamic was shaped by a likely early breakaway, an intermediate sprint at Maussane-les-Alpilles, a categorised climb at Col de la Vayède, then a compelling battle of the sprinters' trains on the run-in to Montpellier.

HOW IT UNFOLDED / A largely nervy day, with lots of pushing and shoving between the fast men wanting a clean sprint and the GC riders fighting to maintain position. The dreaded Mistral winds threatened to split the peloton apart. Luis Maté ventured up the road from the off but was engulfed after 44km. The bunch remained intact until the closing stages, when the fireworks started.

A wheel change in the final hour dashed Sagan's hopes of a first stage win.

Cavendish crashed 30km from home. Both managed to get back into contention as the race swept into Montpellier, but Greipel proved fastest in the final burst.

Boasson Hagen moved up to second place after finishing 12th in the flat-out finale. Froome coasted home safely in 18th position alongside the other GC contenders. 'It's been a stressful week, but good at the same time,' he said. 'We've come through it well as a team and we're sitting in a good position now heading into the Pyrenees.'

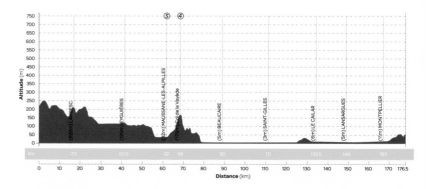

Stage 6
UPS AND DOWNS
Thursday 4 July / Aix-en-Provence to Montpellier, 176.5km

ROUTE / The race approaches the Pyrenees via the vineyards of the Hérault with four intermediate climbs – a one–two punch in the form of the Col des 13 Vents and the Col de la Croix de Mounis, and a second set in the Tarn. A downhill run to the finish appealed to the sprinters as a final flourish before the mountain stages.

HOW IT UNFOLDED / The day looked set to produce an intriguing battle between attackers and sprinters. As a crash blocked the road and disrupted the peloton, a two-man breakaway disappeared until the thigh-sapping Col de la Croix de Mounis proved to be decisive, and the race split into three groups.

With Mark Cavendish, André Greipel and Marcel Kittel all well back, Cannondale arrived at the front to string things out for Peter Sagan. The Slovak was able to take maximum points at the

intermediate sprint before a counter-attack from the pack as former leader Jan Bakelants and two others went up the road. Spirits were broken as the climbs continued and the second breakaway was finally reeled in with 3km to go. Sagan rewarded his team's hard work with the stage win.

Chris Froome and Team Sky occupied a prominent position throughout the stage. Froome and Richie Porte finished in a strong position overall, 8 seconds back on the yellow jersey.

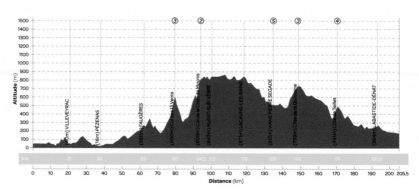

Stage 7
RUGGED COUNTRY
Friday 5 July / Montpellier to Albi, 205.5km

ROUTE / The first big GC shaker. The stage was dominated by the final pair of climbs: the *hors catégorie* hairpin drag up the Col de Pailhères, where long, high-gradient sections pruned the peloton before the riders plummeted down the descent ahead of the daunting Ax 3 Domaines summit finish.

HOW IT UNFOLDED / The peloton allowed four men – including Christophe Riblon, who won on Ax 3 Domaines in 2010 – to forge ahead before Team Sky and Orica-GreenEDGE began to combine at the front, with Geraint Thomas swapping off in rotation with the team of outgoing race leader Daryl Impey.

After the intermediate sprint, won by André Greipel, the GC teams rallied ahead of the 15.3km Col du Pailhères ascent and rival trains formed. Riblon pushed onwards. Robert Gesink and Thomas Voeckler attacked before Nairo Quintana fired clear to crest the climb first.

The peloton followed just over a minute later, with a concerted turn from each and every member of Team Sky. With Quintana overhauled on the final Category-1 ramps, it was left to Chris Froome and Richie Porte to accelerate in an emphatic display of climbing and lead home a Team Sky one–two. Froome's stunning attack in the final 5kms rewarded him with a lead of 51 seconds over his team-mate in the standings for the yellow jersey.

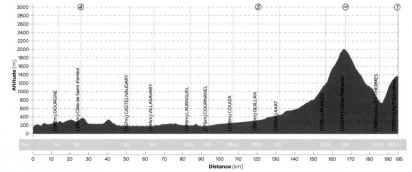

Stage 8
SHOW OF STRENGTH
Saturday 6 July / Castres to Ax 3 Domaines, 195km

ROUTE / A monster stage that featured a relentless barrage of Category-1 climbing, including the Col de Portet d'Aspet, the legendary Col de Peyresourde and La Hourquette d'Ancizan before an intruiging downhill run to the finish.

HOW IT UNFOLDED / The pace was extreme, Peter Kennaugh left the road, and a number of his team-mates slipped back as attacks fired off relentlessly, leaving just Porte and Froome together at the sharp end.

With the Tasmanian unable to hold the pace, Froome took up the running. Team Sky regrouped in the valley and dug in to bridge themselves and Porte across to their isolated leader, but Movistar upped the pace each time the gap dropped, and Porte slipped further off the pace.

With 35km to go, Nairo Quintana unleashed the first of four short attacks. Froome coolly shut down all danger ahead of the long descent to the finish. A slowing in the peloton provided the springboard for Martin and Fuglsang to jump clear.

Froome, having fought a lone battle for 138km against the might of the Movistar and Saxo-Tinkoff teams, demonstrated his brilliance to finish and open out an advantage of 01' 25" over nearest rival Alejandro Valverde heading into the rest day. The stage ended sadly for Team Sky, with Vasili Kiryienka, so integral in helping the team claim yellow, finishing outside the time limit and being forced to abandon.

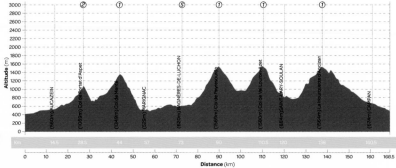

Stage 9
RESILIENT IN YELLOW

Sunday 7 July / Saint-Girons to Bagnères-de-Bigorre, 168.5km

ROUTE / Not pan-flat, with gently undulating roads and the Category-4 climb of the Côte de Dinan, but the route into Brittany offered nothing to thwart a dramatic bunch finish.

HOW IT UNFOLDED / Fresh after the rest day, the riders maintained an average speed of 44 km/h to keep tabs on a five-man getaway. Team Sky assumed a position at the head of the pack, with David López sharing turns at the front with the sprint teams to ensure the quintet's lead never stretched beyond five minutes.

Greipel outpaced Sagan in the intermediate sprint. Tension increased as the race turned on to the coastline in the last 20km, but Froome was well positioned to avoid any crosswind splits. Superbly marshalled by Ian Stannard and Edvald Boasson Hagen at the climax, he crossed the line as Marcel Kittel narrowly pipped Greipel to victory.

Kittel's team-mate Tom Veelers was sent tumbling in the last 100m after peeling off into Mark Cavendish's sprint line and then being clipped as the Manxman produced his final kick for the line.

There was no change in the GC standings.

STAGE 10 RESULT:

Winner. Marcel Kittel (Ger); Argos-Shimano; 04h 53' 25"

2. André Greipel (Ger); Lotto-Belisol; @ same time

3. Mark Cavendish (GB); Omega Pharma-Quick Step; @ same time

OVERALL STANDINGS:

1. Christopher Froome (GB); Team Sky; 41h 52' 43"

2. Alejandro Valverde (Esp); Movistar; 01' 25"

3. Bauke Mollema (Ned); Belkin; +01' 44"

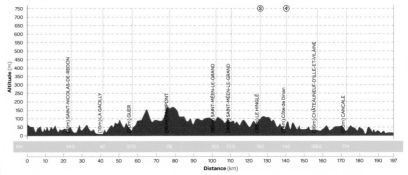

Stage 10
SPRINT SKIRMISHES
Tuesday 9 July / Saint-Gildas-des-Bois to Saint-Malo, 197km

ROUTE / A rolling opening half levelled out for a flat run to the finish line on the coast. Not a particularly technical course, with only a few tight corners – the most testing being a sharp right-hander around 2km from the end – but the second half of the course ran parallel to the picturesque coastline and then turned towards it, so the wind posed potential problems.

HOW IT UNFOLDED / Riders rolled down the start ramp in near-perfect conditions. Canadian veteran Svein Tuft, Thomas De Gendt of Belgium and the German world champion Tony Martin set early markers.

Martin's advantage of 1 minute 1 second over De Gendt stood for more than four hours until the last rider, one Christopher Froome, scoured his way efficiently around the course to pip De Gendt with 47 seconds to spare and finish 12 seconds behind Martin.

The Team Sky leader's advantage at the top of the overall standings extended to 3 minutes 25 seconds. Alejandro Valverde's 13th place saw him retain second spot, although his advantage over Bauke Mollema dropped to just 12 seconds after the Dutchman came home in 11th.

Richie Porte sealed a fantastic top-four finish, with Kanstantsin Siutsou, Team Sky's third-fastest rider, clocking the 32nd-fastest time as he and the remainder of the team chose to conserve their energies for the bigger tests to come.

STAGE 11 RESULT:

Winner. Tony Martin (Ger); Omega Pharma-Quick Step; 36' 29"

2. Christopher Froome (GB); Team Sky; +00' 12"

3. Thomas De Gendt (Bel); Vacansoleil-DCM; +01' 01"

OVERALL STANDINGS:

1. Christopher Froome (GB); Team Sky; 42h 29' 24"

2. Alejandro Valverde (Esp); Movistar; +03' 25"

3. Bauke Mollema (Ned); Belkin; +03' 37"

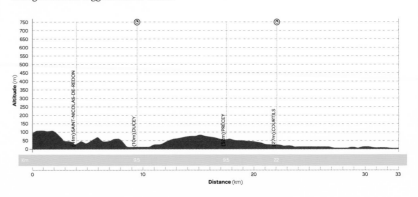

Stage 11
STORMING DISPLAY
Wednesday 10 July / Avranches to Mont-Saint-Michel, 33km, Individual Time Trial

Another one for the sprinters. The route travelled south-east towards the centre of France with no categorised climbs, but plenty of short, sharp rises dotted along a gently undulating course. As they crossed the Loire, the riders needed to be wary of a series of technical corners inside the final 2km, which threatened a hectic finale.

HOW IT UNFOLDED/ Under overcast skies, a five-man escape party attempted an unlikely breakaway on a day when the sprinters were eyeing up their chances from the off. The sprint outfits joined Team Sky at the front to control the stage as they chased down the quintet.

With the sprint bearing down, the final man was caught just 6.2km from the finish line. Team Sky arrived at the front with Thomas leading the line. With the help of Stannard, Froome steered clear of trouble in the collision-marred climax to retain yellow, but Boasson Hagen was a victim of a high-speed crash with just under 3km to go. He was forced to abandon the race with a fractured upper arm and right scapula, reducing Froome's guardians to six, including two debutants and a rider with a cracked pelvis.

In a thrilling finish Kittel burst past a bewildered Cavendish to win by half a wheel. The GC standings were unaffected.

STAGE 12 RESULT:
Winner. Marcel Kittel (Ger); Argos-Shimano; 04h 49' 49"
2. Mark Cavendish (GB); Omega Pharma-Quick Step; @ same time
3. Peter Sagan (Svk); Cannondale; @ same time
OVERALL STANDINGS:
1. Christopher Froome (GB); Team Sky; 47h 19' 13"
2. Alejandro Valverde (Esp); Movistar; +03' 25"
3. Bauke Mollema (Ned); Belkin; +03' 37"

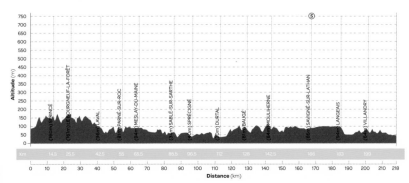

Stage 12
SPRINT SHOWDOWN
Thursday 11 July / Fougères to Tours, 218km

ROUTE/ The race continued to move south-east, with another largely flat day punctuated by a challenging short, sharp climb up from Bruère-Allichamps, 10km from the finish. The rise was a potential hindrance to sprint trains, providing a platform for solo attackers to go for it. With a straight run-in, the sprint trains that prevailed over the climb would make a full-throttle dash for the line.

HOW IT UNFOLDED/ Six riders sped up the road in what looked like a textbook stage for sprinters. All plans changed when cross-winds split the race in half with 112kms remaining. An upturn of pace from Omega Pharma–Quick Step caused chaos as echelons formed and panic ensued. Kittel was a casualty. Valverde suffered a mechanical that would lose him over eight minutes. Belkin added their impetus to the chase.

With 31 km to go, Contador's Saxo-Tinkoff team hit the front to string out an already stretched race and heap pressure on Team Sky. Froome found himself distanced. Stannard, Thomas, Siutsou and Kennaugh worked hard, seeking to limit the losses of their leader. Cavendish held off Sagan in a 14-man group sprint to emerge with his second stage victory.

Froome lost over a minute, but still ended the day with a decent advantage over Mollema before the race headed into the mountains.

STAGE 13 RESULT:
Winner. Mark Cavendish (GB); Omega Pharma-Quick Step; 03h 40' 08"
2. Peter Sagan (Svk); Cannondale; @ same time
3. Bauke Mollema (Ned); Belkin; @ same time
OVERALL STANDINGS:
1. Christopher Froome (GB); Team Sky; 51h 00' 30"
2. Bauke Mollema (Ned); Belkin; +02' 28"
3. Alberto Contador (Esp); Saxo-Tinkoff; +02' 45"

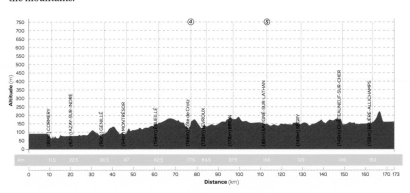

Stage 13
TESTING TIMES

Friday 12 July / Tours to Saint-Amand-Montrond, 173km

ROUTE / A generous smattering of notable climbs – two Category-3s and five Category-4s – served as a challenging hors d'oeuvre to the critical mountain stages ahead. The route undulated from the off, tailor-made for a breakaway. The meaty section of the stage would be the arduous climbs of the Côte de Thizy-les-Bourgs (at 113km) and Col du Pilon (at 126.5km), followed by a speedy 25km descent.

HOW IT UNFOLDED / An 18-man escape group battled it out but the peloton, mindful of Mont Ventoux waiting the next day, was happy to let the attackers go clear. Team Sky set a manageable tempo at the front on behalf of the *maillot jaune*. It was a pacy start to the day but, courtesy of his team-mates, Froome enjoyed an armchair ride to the finish, the peloton cruising in 7 minutes and 16 seconds down on the day's winner.

Within the final 20km the escapees began attacking one another. Julien Simon tried to make it a stage victory for France but Matteo Trentin of Italy stunned the crowds in Lyons by hitting out on the home straight to take the biggest win of his career.

The GC standings remained the same as the race moved into the Alps.

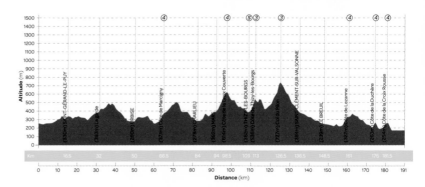

Stage 14
EASY DOES IT
Saturday 13 July / Saint-Pourçain-sur-Sioule to Lyons, 191km

ROUTE / An epic day. The road undulated south for 208km into Provence, taking in three Category-4 climbs and a Category-3 climb before reaching Malaucène. It then wound east to the foot of the iconic and punishing climb to the finish line atop the exposed moonscape of Mont Ventoux (21km long, average gradient 7.5 per cent, maximum gradient 12 per cent).

HOW IT UNFOLDED / Bastille Day inspired the French riders to flex muscle at the front. After a pacy first hour, a ten-man group was allowed to go clear by the peloton. Following the intermediate sprint, Team Sky hit the front with a superb display – Thomas, Stannard, López and Siutsou all pushing hard as the race hit the lower slopes of the *hors catégorie* Ventoux. Kennaugh's turn set a strong tempo to peg back the attack of Nairo Quintana, before Porte took over.

The Tasmanian's attack destroyed an already depleted peloton, with only Froome and Alberto Contador able to hold his wheel. With 7.2km to go and Porte's effort over, Froome unleashed a powerful attack to bridge across to Quintana's lone attack and forge onwards to distance all rivals and become the first British victor on the Ventoux. He won by a stunning 29 seconds, extending his race lead to 4 minutes and 14 seconds and reclaiming the polka dot jersey in the process.

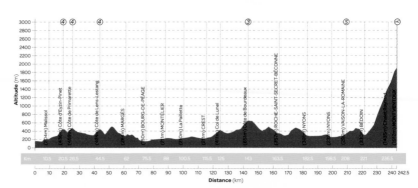

Stage 15
TOP OF THE WORLD

Sunday 14 July / Givors to Mont Ventoux, 242.5km

ROUTE / A picturesque path through cliff-lined valleys and over testing passes included three categorised climbs: Category-3 Côte de la Montagne de Bluye rolled into the demanding Category-2 Col de Macuègne, followed by a near 100km sector to Gap, before the flick north-east for an ascent of the Col de Manse and a frantic descent to the finish.

HOW IT UNFOLDED / With the allure of a breakaway win – and a potential gap-creating impact on the GC – the stage got off to an intense start with Sagan, Valverde and Daniel Martin attempting to escape. Team Sky eventually allowed 26 riders up the road. The breakaway was 8 minutes ahead when the peloton was halted at a rail crossing, and more than 12 minutes clear as they tackled the final climb. Two riders from the breakaway attacked, but were passed first by Adam Hansen, then Rui Costa, who descended alone to take the stage win.

Back in the peloton, Siutsou, Kennaugh and Porte set a furious pace on the Col de Manse. Froome was one of only eight riders left in the pack over the climb, but had to unclip his foot on the descent to the finish after Alberto Contador overcooked a corner immediately in front of him, which forced both riders into an abrupt and untimely halt. Porte reacted swiftly and paced Froome back to his closest rivals to maintain his overall advantage.

STAGE 16 RESULT:

Winner. Rui Costa (Por); Movistar; 03h 52' 45"
2. Christophe Riblon (Fra); Ag2r-La Mondiale; +00' 42"
3. Arnold Jeannesson (Fra); FDJ.fr; +00' 42"

OVERALL STANDINGS:

1. Christopher Froome (GB); Team Sky; 65h 15' 36"
2. Bauke Mollema (Ned); Belkin; +04' 14"
3. Alberto Contador (Esp); Saxo-Tinkoff; +04' 25"

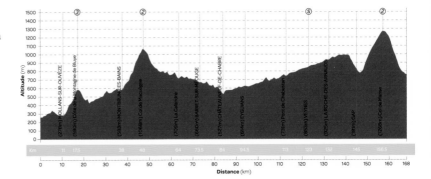

Stage 16
DOWNHILL DRAMA
Tuesday 16 July / Vaison-la-Romaine to Gap, 168km

ROUTE / A tough course featured two Category-2 climbs – the Côte de Puy-Sanières and the Côte de Réallon – and a twisty and technical latter two-thirds. All eyes were on the clouds, as the descents would prove treacherous in wet conditions.

HOW IT UNFOLDED / The early marker was set by Lieuwe Westra with a time of 54 minutes and 2 seconds, which world champion Tony Martin could not match. Two hours later Jon Izagirre was the first rider to dip below 54 minutes with 53 minutes and 58 seconds. A further hour passed before Tejay van Garderen cruised home with 14 seconds to spare.

Rain threatened to affect the big hitters, but Valverde posted a time 1 minute and 21 seconds faster than Van Garderen. Andrew Talansky, Michal Kwiatkowski and Joaquim Rodríguez all went quicker, before Contador proved the man to beat as Froome began his run.

The Team Sky leader trailed Contador by 20 seconds at the second time split, but brought that back to within 11 seconds at the third check after swapping his road bike for a time-trial machine. Froome tucked into his aero position and surged home in a time of 51 minutes 33 seconds for a third stage win and an increased lead in the GC. Contador's performance ensured that he climbed one place to second overall, 17 seconds ahead of Saxo-Tinkoff team-mate Roman Kreuziger in third.

STAGE 17 RESULT:

Winner. Christopher Froome (GB); Team Sky; 0h 51' 33"
2. Alberto Contador (Esp); Saxo-Tinkoff; +00' 09"
3. Joaquim Rodríguez (Esp); Katusha; +00' 10"

OVERALL STANDINGS:

1. Christopher Froome (GB); Team Sky; 66h 07' 09"
2. Alberto Contador (Esp); Saxo-Tinkoff; +04' 34"
3. Roman Kreuziger (Cze); Saxo-Tinkoff; +04' 51"

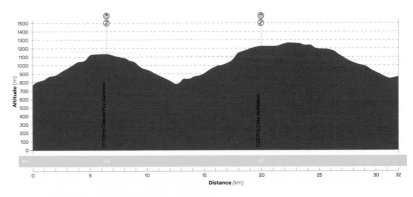

Stage 17
QUICKEST OF ALL

Wednesday 17 July / Embrun to Chorges, 32km, Individual Time Trial

ROUTE / Another epic stage, which sent the riders twice up the legendary Alpe d'Huez. Those daunting hairpins came after a bruising opening 108km containing two Category-2 climbs and a Category-3 ascent. After reaching the summit, the riders wound up the Category-2 Col de Sarenne and then flew down into the valley, before tackling the Alpe d'Huez again.

HOW IT UNFOLDED / As the race left Gap, Movistar and Saxo-Tinkoff ignited the anticipated GC battles as they looked to launch men up the road. Froome came to the fore to shut down attacks himself. A breakaway of nine was allowed up the road as Thomas and Stannard combined to drive the peloton towards the first passage over the famous Alpe, with Siutsou and López taking over through the wall of fans on the climb.

Contador and Kreuziger used the descent as a springboard to open up a gap. First Kennaugh, then Movistar arrived at the front to shut things down before the final ascent. Porte valiantly bridged across to pace Froome all the way to the finish. Froome was later docked 20 seconds for taking an energy gel in the closing stages. He dropped 1 minute 6 seconds to Quintana but still extended his race lead to 5 minutes and 11 seconds.

The day was special for Christophe Riblon, who ended the French wait for a stage victory.

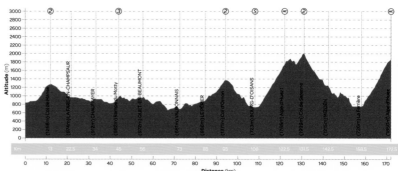

Stage 18
RUNNING ON EMPTY
Thursday 18 July / Gap to Alpe-d'Huez, 172.5km

ROUTE / Another leg- and lung-buster of a day, with back-to-back *hors catégorie* climbs (the Col du Glandon and Col de la Madeleine), two Category-1 ascents and one Category-2 incline to surmount. The early climbs each came with a long and testing descent for good measure before the route rose three more times ahead of the dash downhill to the finish.

HOW IT UNFOLDED / Ryder Hesjedal and Jon Izagirre led a 44-strong group of escapees on a day in which long-range breakaway experts fancied their chances. The gap opened out on the Glandon as Team Sky's Thomas and Stannard returned to pace-setting duties at the front of the bunch.

On the descent off the Madeleine, Contador's Saxo-Tinkoff team moved up to push the tempo along the valley floor and on to the undulating run-in. A hard pace followed on the final climbs, thinning

out the group before the final descent, but sustained attacks from Froome's GC rivals did not materialise.

The stage win belonged to Rui Costa, after the Portuguese rider hit out on the lower slopes of the final climb and powered past his fellow escapees to claim his second victory of the race. Froome, 8 minutes and 40 seconds further back and part of a group that was awarded the same time in Le Grand-Bornand, thus maintained his lead over nearest rival Contador.

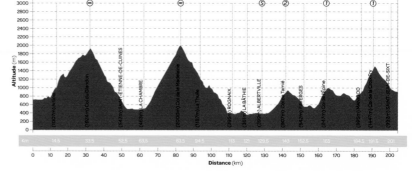

Stage 19
PHEW, THAT'S OVER
Friday 19 July / Bourg-d'Oisans to Le Grand-Bornand, 204.5km

ROUTE / Starting and finishing on the western banks of Lake Annecy, the penultimate day's route tested tired legs with four climbs before the potentially stage-deciding duo of the Category-1 Mont Revard and the *hors catégorie* summit finish on Annecy-Semnoz.

HOW IT UNFOLDED / Ten riders combined early in a break, but a galvanised Movistar squad kept them on a short leash, pegging the gap at around 1 minute. Pierre Rolland racked up 10 mountain points, briefly moving into the lead of the polka dot jersey competition.

Tejay van Garderen bridged across the gap as Movistar slackened off the chase, but business soon picked up as the peloton approached the final climb. A brave solo bid from Jens Voigt was reeled in on the steep slopes with 8.5km to go, as the main contenders hit the front. Alberto Contador foundered and disappeared from contention. Froome, supported by Stannard, Thomas, Siutsou, López and finally Porte, unleashed a powerful acceleration to close in on Rodríguez and Quintana, the trio each claiming a place on the final podium.

Victory for Quintana secured the Colombian the polka dot jersey at the expense of Froome, in addition to the white young rider's jersey, but it was the elated Team Sky leader who clenched his fist as the winner elect of this year's race.

STAGE 20 RESULT:

Winner. Nairo Quintana (Col); Movistar; 03hr 39' 04"

2. Joaquim Rodríguez (Esp); Katusha; +00' 18"

3. Christopher Froome (GB); Team Sky; +00' 29"

OVERALL STANDINGS:

1. Christopher Froome (GB); Team Sky; 80h 49' 33"

2. Nairo Quintana (Col); Movistar; +05' 03"

3. Joaquim Rodríguez (Esp); Katusha; +5' 47"

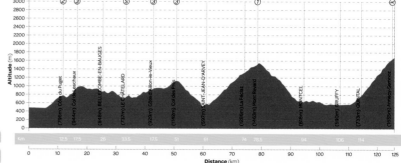

Stage 20
LAST DAY IN THE ALPS
Saturday 20 July / Annecy to Annecy-Semnoz, 125km

ROUTE / The final stage was set for the Tour's traditional processional celebration turned frantic sprint for glory on the Champs-Elysées. This year, to mark the 100th edition, the riders entered Paris at sunset and rode the final ten laps under lights.

HOW IT UNFOLDED / Soon after the afternoon start in Versailles, Froome dropped back to the team car to enjoy a glass of champagne as Team Sky passed out the bubbly on the run. Froome, Porte, Kennaugh, Stannard, Thomas, López and Siutsou hit the front to lead the peloton on to the Champs-Elysées and around the Arc de Triomphe for the first time as the sun began to set over Paris.

As expected, a number of attackers tried to go clear – David Millar, then Alejandro Valverde, Bram Tankink and Manuel Quinziato – as the sprinters' teams controlled things behind.

As the bell rang for the final lap, Team Sky hit the front, with Thomas leading the peloton across the line with the victorious yellow jersey in second wheel. Then it was left to the sprinters. Marcel Kittel edged out a close three-man sprint to round off the centenary edition in style. Moments later, an emotional Froome crossed the line arm in arm with his teammates, having secured back-to-back Tour victories for Great Britain and Team Sky.

STAGE 21 RESULT:

Winner. Marcel Kittel (Ger); Argos-Shimano; 03h 06' 14"

2. André Greipel (Ger); Lotto-Belisol; @ same time

3. Mark Cavendish (GB); Omega Pharma-Quick Step; @ same time

OVERALL STANDINGS:

1. Christopher Froome (GB); Team Sky; 83h 56' 40"

2. Nairo Quintana (Col); Movistar; + 04' 20"

3. Joaquim Rodriquez (Esp); Katusha; +05' 04"

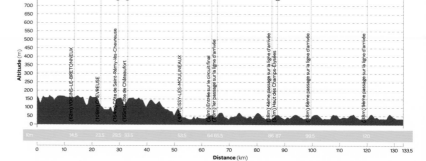

Stage 21
FABULOUS FROOME

Sunday 21 July / Versailles to Paris, 118km

First published in 2013 by
HarperSport
an imprint of HarperCollinsPublishers
77–85 Fulham Palace Road,
Hammersmith, London W6 8JB
www.harpercollins.co.uk

10 9 8 7 6 5 4 3 2 1

Photographs by Scott Mitchell
Words by Sarah Edworthy
Design by Martin Topping

A catalogue record of this book is available from the
British Library

ISBN 978-0-00-754471-4

Printed and bound in the United Kingdom by CPI Colour

MIX
Paper from
responsible sources
FSC www.fsc.org   **FSC® C007454**

FSC™ is a non-profit international organisation established to promote the
responsible management of the world's forests. Products carrying the FSC
label are independently certified to assure consumers that they come from
forests that are managed to meet the social, economic and ecological needs
of present and future generations, and other controlled sources.

Find out more about HarperCollins and the environment at
www.harpercollins.co.uk/green